Housing New York

Housing New York

Policy Challenges and Opportunities

Michael J. Wolkoff

State University of New York Press

AJP 0459-0/2

Published by
State University of New York Press, Albany

© 1990 State University of New York

For information, address State University of New York
Press, State University Plaza, Albany, N.Y., 12246

Library of Congress Cataloging-in-Publication Data

Wolkoff, Michael J.
    Housing New York : policy challenges and opportunities / Michael
Wolkoff.
        p.   cm.
    Includes bibliographical references (p.   ).
    ISBN 0-7914-0353-X. — ISBN 0-7914-0354-8 (pbk.)
    1. Housing—New York (State) 2. Housing policy—New York (State)
I. Title.
HD7303.N7W65 1990
363.5'8'09747—dc20   89-28081
                                                               CIP

10 9 8 7 6 5 4 3 2 1

For my daughter,
Julia Gayle Wolkoff

Contents

List of Figures

List of Figures

List of Tables

Acknowledgments

I would like to thank a number of friends and colleagues whose contributions made this work possible. I owe Bruce Jacobs a special vote of thanks. Bruce's contribution extends far beyond his excellent chapter on housing the elderly, which has been included in this volume. Without his diligent editing and expert advice, this book would have been far less interesting. I am also grateful for the help of Jeryl Mumpower, of the Rockefeller Institute of Government. Jeryl had the foresight and wisdom to fund an earlier version of this project as one of the New York State Project 2000 reports. His interest and support over the last three years made the transition from research outline to book possible.

A number of other colleagues also made important contributions. Eric Hanushek provided useful, detailed comments on earlier drafts of the manuscript and encouraged me to seek a wider audience. His advice was extremely valuable. Johnny Yinger provided useful suggestions at an early stage of the process, and his insights helped shape the final manuscript. Russell Roberts and David Weimer proved to be supportive colleagues, and I would like to acknowledge their influence in shaping my discussion of rent controls.

I was also fortunate to have a number of able research assistants. I would like to thank Sharon McGroder, Marge Frohm, Paul Janaskie, Annette Steinacker, Kirk Won and Brigid Handy for their help. Dana Loud provided excellent secretarial assistance.

Finally, and most of all, I would like to thank my wife, Karen Altman. Her support and patience ultimately made this work possible.

1

Introduction

For the vast majority of Americans, the American dream has been realized. The continuous, steady improvement in living conditions has left most households better housed than ever before. But, unfortunately, not all Americans have shared in this good fortune. For an increasing segment of our country's population, the dream of home ownership, or the opportunity to live in adequate, affordable housing appears further and further away.

Perhaps, the most disturbing symbol of this problem is the homeless men, women, and children living in the streets of America. But, in fact, the homeless are but a tip of the affordable housing iceberg. Excessive shelter costs are borne by over three-quarters of the 13 million American households with income below the poverty line.[1] And, the poor are not alone in facing the financial burdens imposed by high housing costs. Many newly formed households, single-headed families, and elderly households face affordability problems where none before existed.

Housing affordability problems have united poor households facing severe financial hardship with emerging young households who find it difficult to obtain the shelter equivalent to what their parents enjoyed.[2] This coalition has been effective in calling attention to housing-related issues. After almost a decade of relative inactivity, the federal government has been summoned to provide leadership in setting housing policy.

Ironically, demands for national policy solutions for housing affordability problems have occurred when the prospect that federal policy makers will pursue new initiatives is *de minimus*. Policy makers are reluctant to champion new programs in the context of large budgetary deficits and robust political resistance to tax increases. The late 1980s and early 1990s are not the time for launching new program ventures.

Washington's reluctance to initiate new programs does not stem from budgetary concerns alone. Over the past two decades, expectations about appropriate activities for different levels of government have changed. Now, state and local governments are expected to play an increasingly important role in policy formulation and implementation. This is particularly true in the case of housing policy, where sub-federal units of government have an essential interest.

In addition, recent events have shaken our trust in the ability of federal institutions to reach housing policy goals. The near bankruptcy of thousands of savings and loan institutions and the proposed bailout by the federal government leaves many observers questioning the wisdom of expanding federal influence in the credit markets. Recent revelations about improprieties at HUD raise further questions about the prudence of undertaking new programs under the leadership of the federal housing agency.

There is much to gain by looking beyond the federal government for housing policy leadership and guidance. Housing markets are local in structure, and state and local governments are well situated to design effective policy responses to specific local conditions. National efforts may fail to recognize the underlying conditions of distinctive submarkets. State and local governments already have a major influence on housing markets. Zoning, taxation, and regulatory policies made at the state house or local town hall all have important impacts on private actors making housing decisions. Any policy suggestions along these dimensions will need to recognize state and local governmental interests.

Finally, state and local governments have become more resourceful in responding to policy problems. States are increasingly being viewed as laboratories where public policy experimentation can take place. Identifying new solutions to housing problems requires that we turn from a federal perspective and examine what is happening in the states.

In this book we conduct an in-depth examination of the housing market conditions and policies in one state—New York. New York has long been a leader in policy innovations. Although New York cannot be considered a typical state, its diversity and range of housing choices and problems incorporate the range of situations found in many other states. New York's activist approach to problem solving makes it an excellent laboratory to examine.

Understanding New York's housing markets and how policy makers respond to housing problems will lend insights into other states' activities, as well as inform national policy choices. There is much to be learned from the New York State experience. To echo the sentiments of a song made popular by Frank Sinatra, ". . . if you can make it there [New York], you can make it anywhere."

Housing issues lie at the core of the policy agenda facing New York State in the coming decades. Housing consumption is a major element of the quality of life of New York State's residents. The attractiveness of New York as a place to live and do business, and its ability to compete in the markets of the next century, will depend, in part, on the availability of decent, affordable housing for the state's work force.

For most New Yorkers, the goals of the 1949 Housing Act, ". . . a decent home and suitable living environment for every American family...," have been achieved. New Yorkers face the arrival of the 21st century better housed than ever before; more people own their homes, both rental and ownership housing conditions have improved in quality, and fewer people live in crowded conditions. Yet, despite the appreciable improvement in housing quality, not all state residents are "adequately" housed, nor is housing available at prices that all "can afford."

The visible presence of the homeless living in the streets of our major cities, the existence of dilapidated trailer homes in rural New York, and the large percentage of poor people paying excessive portions of their income for housing services, are evidence that not all New Yorkers enjoy and share in the general improvement in housing quality. Even for those in New York State with adequate housing, shelter often can only be obtained at greater and greater financial sacrifice. For some groups, the cost of adequate housing leaves room for little else in the houshold budget.

The concern for adequate, affordable housing is not merely held by those residents who are poorly housed, living in deteriorating neighborhoods, or facing excessive housing costs. This concern is shared by many, more affluent New Yorkers. Paradoxically, concerns about access to adequate, affordable housing are held at the same time that housing ownership has brought new-found wealth to so many. Homeowners on Long Island, cooperative apartment owners in Manhattan, and suburban residents of metropolitan Albany can marvel at rapidly increasing housing prices and the wealth that property ownership has brought them, while at the same time worrying whether their children can afford to live nearby. Young families living in cramped quarters wonder if any larger apartments exist in the virtually vacancy-free, rent-regulated market of New York City. Employers ponder how they can attract moderate wage workers, vital for keeping their industries competitive, when housing prices within reasonable commuting distance are so high.

While many New Yorkers share the concern for the poorly housed, it is vital to recognize two general propositions. First, the private housing market has worked for the majority of New Yorkers. Attempts at solving perceived housing problems should studiously avoid disrupting the well-functioning part of the market. Second, New York State's housing problems cannot be solved easily. Housing market outcomes are the consequence of the activities of many different actors, only somewhat susceptible to governmental suasion. Further, the state can improve existing housing conditions or ease the affordability problems many households face, only at the expense of other goals. The fundamental question facing residents of this state is how much of the state's resources should be directed towards housing, and what form should housing policy take?

The approach of the year 2000 provides a natural opportunity for policy makers to step back and assess the conditions of today's housing market and anticipate the challenges that will shape the future. This study examines the opportunities and constraints facing New York State housing policy makers as we approach the 21st century. Virtually no generalizations apply to all of the state's housing markets. But there are a sufficient number of common threads for us to identify key issue areas and to develop an agenda for future policy actions.

It is inconceivable that any document could analyze, let alone solve, the state's housing problems. Many of the issues addressed in this study appear insolvable. Others will defy solution because of the inability of decision makers to reach consensus, in no small part because each policy choice creates winners and losers. A goal of this project is to provide a foundation from which future housing discussions can proceed.

Chapter 2 of the book examines New York State's role in housing policy. Not all housing issues are under the state's province, nor should they be. In many instances the actions of private developers, individual consumers, or local officials will overwhelm any action the state might take. Even where the state has clear lines of authority, not all desirable policy options should be pursued. There are too few resources for all projects, and those that are undertaken must be understood to be at the expense of other worthy claims on the public's resources.

In the third chapter of this book I examine the existing housing conditions in the state with the intent of identifying areas of concern or promise. Detailed analysis is presented of housing conditions by tenure status, region, and race. The analysis shows housing affordability to be the crucial policy issue facing New York State. In chapter 4, I conduct an in-depth analysis of the affordability problem. This analysis provides detailed estimates of the gap between household income and housing costs in New York State.

Chapter 5 examines New York City's rent regulations and their impact. Chapter 6 looks at a number of changes and trends that are likely to affect policy making over the next decade. Key among them is the changing demographic structure in the state. The next 15 years will see a significant aging of the state's population, the likely continued decline in the size of the typical household, and the continued emergence of female-headed households. Each of these trends has important implications for how the state's housing markets function.

Chapter 7 analyzes a number of housing policy options that the state can pursue to alleviate housing market problems. I examine both demand and supply-side strategies and evaluate the potential of state efforts to influence housing market outcomes. This chapter also contains an analysis of the impact of rent regulations on New York City's housing market and offers a number of suggestions for easing the heavy hand of regulation.

Chapter 8 contains a detailed analysis of the housing situation of the aged by Dr. Bruce Jacobs. The aged are the fastest growing component of the state's population and have a particular set of housing requirements distinguishing them from other subgroups. Chapter 9 presents conclusions and some suggestions for general policy guidance.

2

Defining the State's Role in Housing

The vast majority of New Yorkers live in housing provided by the private sector, without direct government subsidy. For the majority of these households, the private market works remarkably well. But for many, including the poor, younger households and some members of minority groups, the functioning of the private housing market results in poor quality housing at too high a price.

Governmental housing policy is best understood as a response to (and at times a cause of) limitations and movements in private market forces. The social implications of individuals' housing choices have long been considered an issue of governmental concern, because private housing decisions almost always disregard public repercussions. Private decisions about housing investment, maintenance, abandonment, and sales are all generally made irrespective of their social consequences. Further, a significant number of Americans believe that all citizens should have access to an adequate and affordable home. For many, providing housing assistance is a palatable way of altering the income distribution.

To counter any potential private market failure, and to rectify socially unacceptable outcomes resulting from the existing distribution of income, a variety of housing policy initiatives have been developed by all levels of government.[3] The extent to which different levels of government have participated in housing policy has varied over time, reflecting changing conceptions of federalism and budgetary exigencies.

Until most recently, for many years the state had played a supporting role in a cast dominated by federal and local actors. This had not always been the case. Prior to the 1930s, the federal government was only tangentially involved in housing. What little housing policy there was originated at the state or local level of government.

All this changed when federal housing initiatives (aimed at improving the living conditions of the poor, redeveloping neighborhoods, or stabilizing the macroeconomy) assumed the predominant role in determining the public production and subsidy of housing. The federal government became extremely active in encouraging and subsidizing housing production by developing programs to insure or provide low-cost mortgage financing for new homeowners. The federal government induced additional housing consumption through the preferential tax treatment of home ownership. The federal government has also provided rental assistance, in the form of direct rental subsidies and the production of public housing, enabling poor and moderate income households to obtain higher quality housing than they could otherwise afford.[4]

Local governments have played a very different role by shaping the form and location of private development. Rather than serving as the engine for housing development, many localities have sought to control its shape, size, and form. Localities have controlled development in their communities, most commonly through the use of detailed local zoning codes. Local activity has been more extensive in the state's more urbanized areas, where the visible presence of dilapidated housing and the homeless has evoked local policy responses.

Amidst all this, the state has served in an intermediary role, extending federal programs, administering intergovernmental grants, coordinating local activities, and centralizing information gathering. New York State housing policies have expanded upon a number of federal programs by increasing their scope and providing benefits to groups otherwise ineligible for federal subsidies, although not every household in need has been helped.

Consider the important extensions in program support for low-income households. State public housing projects housed over 66,000 low-income families in 1985. State supplementation of AFDC payments includes housing assistance payments to poor New Yorkers. The Rural Rental Assistance Program provides direct rental subsidies for low-income elderly and family tenants residing in multifamily projects in rural areas. Home-ownership programs have also been developed for lower income residents through the Housing Trust Fund, thereby providing ownership opportunities to individuals far below the federally set income guidelines.[5]

New York State has also extended federal programs to New York households with incomes too high to qualify for federal assistance. In doing so, the state has chosen to spend its limited budget dollars on groups that aren't most in need. One example is the increase in affordable housing opportunities for middle and moderate income families. The state Mitchell-Lama projects, housing over 100,000 households, extended the range of subsidized households further up the income scale than federal eligibility limits would allow for rental programs. Similarly, the availability of State of New York Mortgage Agency (SONYMA) low-cost mortgages, made possible through its tax-exempt borrowing authority, enabled a wider range of participants to achieve the goal of home ownership than would have been possible under existing private or federal opportunities. These state initiatives have reached many moderate-income renters and homeowners who had been ignored by federal programs.

In other instances, the state has played a coordinating role for federal programs. New York's Housing Finance Agency (HFA) was able to develop low-income housing by tying in with the federal government's Section 8 Program which subsidizes rents in the private market. The end of all new Section 8 funding pulled the financing pin out from these arrangements and forced HFA to reduce its commitments to constructing low-income housing. Similarly, the creation of low-income, multifamily rental units by the Urban Development Corporation was curtailed when the federal Section 236 program ended.

New York State's integrative role in coordinating the activities of local governmental units can be clearly seen in the adoption of a statewide building code. The establishment of this code has greatly reduced the informational requirements of builders operating in multiple jurisdictions. Similarly, the establishment of statewide technical resource centers has minimized the redundancies of localities reproducing the latest information on new building technologies.

The state's intermediary role in housing policy reflects not only its preferences but also the constraints it faces. Many of the activities that the state could pursue are dependent upon the cooperation of local units of government. This cooperation may require that local governmental units change zoning codes, or that the state legislature pass housing legislation. But local communities base their policy decisions on a much narrower constituency than do statewide officials. As a result, it is often the case that local governments do not share the same policy goals as state officials, making cooperation difficult. Even when broad policy goals are shared, there is often disagreement over policy implementation. Many local officials share the statewide perspective on the need for more low-income housing or more prisons, while at the same time refusing to allow these facilities to be placed in their community. These political factors, even more than resource shortages, can constrain the state's attempts to establish housing policy.

Perhaps the most problematic of these constraints is the difficulty housing advocates encounter in trying to convince suburban governments to alter their zoning codes to allow multifamily housing development. Consider, for example, the Rochester Housing Authority's difficulty finding a suburban location to place low-income housing in 1986-87. Rochester, like other large cities in New York State, has more low-income families than adequate units renting at affordable cost. By late 1986, the waiting list for public housing had grown so long that the Housing Authority closed the list to new applicants, rather than offer a false promise that someday housing would become available.

A small measure of relief would have been provided by a federal decision to fund 50 new units of public housing in Rochester. Unfortunately, finding a site in compliance with federal guidelines requiring that the units be constructed at a location of low minority population proved exceedingly difficult. This requirement effectively precluded virtually all available sites in the City of Rochester. Despite the lengthy waiting list for low-income housing in the region, the small size of the proposed project, and the financing of the project by a third party payer (the federal government), the Rochester Housing Authority was unable to find a suburban jurisdiction willing to provide a site where the housing could be built.

This case vividly portrays the difficulty in coordinating state policy. Housing initiatives aimed at goals and objectives shared by a majority of the state's residents can only proceed with the full cooperation of all affected parties. The situation in Rochester is representative of the potential for policy conflict across the state. In this case, the need for low-income housing was pressing, the units were to be paid by a third party, and major local sponsors of the program actively pushed for its enactment. Yet narrower local interests impeded progress. More generally, housing initiatives often generate perceived costs as well as benefits and are usually resisted by the groups so affected.

Although the state's role in housing policy has traditionally been overshadowed by federal policies, governmental responsibilities are in the process of being redefined.[6] By the 1980s, the significance of state and local housing policy initiatives had been greatly magnified by the withdrawal of the federal government from a major housing policy role. During the Reagan administration, total federal housing authority declined from over $30 billion to $11 billion annually, resulting in housing assistance to New York State declining $7 billion from what it would have been without these budget cuts.

Federal withdrawal from housing programs has created a vacuum for state policy makers to fill. Unlike in the past, when expansive federal policies relieved the political pressures on state governments to provide housing assistance, the current federal retraction has heightened the expectations of state activity. State governments are called on not only to fill policy gaps but, in some instances, to pick up prior commitments.

New York State's Housing Policies

Defining the state's role in housing policy requires that we face two key questions. First, how large a portion of the state's budget should be devoted to housing? Second, how should these housing dollars be spent? Clearly, the answers to these two questions are interrelated. Successful programs make it easier to defend larger budget requests while ineffective programs are vulnerable to budget cuts. Similarly, long-standing programs develop political support that make them difficult to disband, regardless of "success." Nevertheless, it is useful for analytic purposes to separate these two issues.

New York State budgets more money for housing than other states.[7] Recent budget figures for the New York State Division of Housing and Community Renewal (1987 to 1988) reveal a budget of nearly $200 million, of which $40 million was for direct expenditures, $108 million for aid to localities, and $25 million for the Low Income Housing Trust Fund. The state also incurs costs that do not appear in the DHCR budget including over $300 million for the shelter allowance portion of AFDC, as well as additional costs for running the various housing finance agencies (SONYMA, HFA), and for a variety of tax expenditure programs.[8] Whether this is the appropriate level of expenditure will depend on housing market conditions and the state's commitment to solving housing problems.

Whatever the level of expenditures, policy makers must determine how housing dollars should be spent. This decision involves two key aspects. First, decision makers must establish policy objectives. Second, they must determine how these objectives can best be achieved.

An examination of existing state housing policies reveals a variety of policy objectives being pursued. A number of these objectives are defined by problems of private market failure. For instance, dilapidated housing can have deleterious neighborhood effects that may be unimportant to the owners of the structure in disrepair. Thus, policies aimed at neighborhood development and improving housing quality have an underlying social rationale. Similarly, if the pride of home ownership engenders desirable social behavior through better property maintenance and community up-keep, policies aimed at encouraging home ownership will have a public purpose. Finally, to the extent policy makers seek to accomplish redistributional goals through housing assistance, a wide set of housing policies are justified.

Housing programs have also evolved to serve other purposes. These programs often reflect the interconnectedness of housing policy goals and the realities of the legislative process. Some of these programs may lack any discernable social purpose other than to redistribute resources from one group of state residents to another. Others may be aimed at achieving alternative objectives, such as stimulating the building construction industry. This multiplicity of goals makes policy evaluation difficult, but it does give some indication of the complexity of concerns and diversity of interests impinging on housing policy formulation.

To evaluate state housing policies it is useful to categorize existing programs by objectives. These then can be compared with state housing conditions for the purpose of assessing resource allocation choices. State housing policies can be viewed as aiming to achieve the following objectives:[9]

1. a high level of housing production;
2. adequate housing finance;
3. reduced housing costs;
4. attraction of private capital;
5. housing assistance to low- and moderate-income households;
6. housing assistance to elderly households;
7. increased home ownership;
8. improved housing quality;
9. neighborhood development and stabilization.

It is clear from this list that state policy objectives have extended beyond issues of redistribution and market failure. Further, the length of this list suggests that not all programs can serve all objectives. In fact, some of the objectives are logically inconsistent. Attempts at improving housing quality are virtually guaranteed to be incompatible with efforts at containing housing costs. Indeed, almost all of the first nine objectives cannot be achieved without increasing state budget costs.[10]

In Table 1, New York State housing policies are grouped by program objectives.[11] Importantly, most programs can be grouped under more than one category. But categorizing programs by objectives is only the first step in developing effective policies. Housing markets are extremely complex and differ widely across the state. Any public intervention in the housing market will result in market readjustments that are likely to have unanticipated effects. Without detailed studies of the operation and impact of a variety of housing policies, it is extremely difficult to make unequivocal assessments of the relative effectiveness of different approaches, particularly if existing policies pursue multiple goals. Evaluating tradeoffs between programs requires not only an assessment of how

TABLE 1

NEW YORK STATE HOUSING PROGRAMS AND OBJECTIVES

OBJECTIVE	PROGRAM
Housing Production	Public Housing Program Mitchell-Lama Housing Housing New York Fort Drum Impact Region Housing Development Fund Rural Rental Assistance Program
Housing Finance	Housing Finance Agency (HFA) State of New York Mortgage Agency (SONYMA) Urban Development Corporation (UDC)
Reduced Housing Costs	Housing Development Fund Rent Regulations Home Energy Assistance Program SONYMA HFA
Attraction of Private Capital	Tax Abatements Affordable Home Ownership Development
Targeted Assistance to Poor	Low Income Housing Trust Fund Rural Rental Assistance Special Needs Housing Demonstration Program
Targeted Assistance to Aged	Senior Citizen Rent Increase Exemption Program Rural Rental Assistance Rural Aging Services Partnership
Increased Home Ownership	SONYMA Rural Home Ownership Assistance Circuit Breaker
Improved Housing Quality	Rental Rehabilitation Program Public Housing Modernization Program Rural Preservation Building Codes
Neighborhood Development	Neighborhood Preservation Program Urban Initiatives Rural Area Revitalization Self Help Area Revitalization Neighborhood Redevelopment Demonstration

effective policies are at achieving a specific goal, but also a comparison across goals.

This overview of existing state housing policy reveals an incremental process whereby New York State has gradually assumed, or shed, responsibilities for a variety of programs, depending on the commitments and capacity of other governmental and private actors. What direction state policies should now take will depend on the existing set of programs in place and an evaluation of housing market conditions in New York State.

In the following chapters of this book, I examine the conditions of New York's housing markets and a number of strategies for attacking housing problems. A detailed examination of existing conditions and trends will provide the required information base for developing housing policy goals. In a later chapter, I examine the potential of these policies for relieving the housing cost burden and analyze likely program effects. Ultimately, we would like to know which policy options are most cost effective. That is, for a given expenditure, which option produces the most impact. This information must be considered a high priority for housing policy analysts who are to determine the best direction for future New York State housing policy.

3

Housing Conditions in New York State

An analysis of New York State's housing markets properly begins with an examination of existing housing conditions and population characteristics. This study makes use of the 1980 Public Use Microdata Sample (PUMS data), the most comprehensive data source available, consisting of a one percent sample of all New York State households and housing units (over 175,000 records in all).[12] It is the only available data set on which a statewide analysis, at the household or housing unit level, can be performed.

In 1980, New York State contained 17,558,072 people, housed in 6,340,429 housing units. The state's population declined four percent from the level reported in the 1970 Census, but the accompanying nine percent decline in average household size explains why there were actually more households in 1980 than 1970 (see Table 2). The 1985 data indicate that the state population is not longer declining. Based on population estimates of the State Data Center, we project that by the year 2000, 18.5 million people could occupy as many as 8 million households.[13]

TABLE 2

NEW YORK STATE HOUSEHOLD AND POPULATION PROJECTIONS

YEAR	POPULATION	AVERAGE HOUSEHOLD SIZE	# HOUSEHOLDS
1970	18,237,000	3.0	5,935,000
1980	17,558,100	2.77	6,340,429
2000*	18,548,300	2.77	6,696,740
2000**	18,548,300	2.3	8,064,479

*Assumes no change in household size.
**Assumes continued historical decline in household size.

Although it is impossible to provide a description of the conditions of all housing units in the state, it is possible to consider a number of commonly used measures to summarize existing conditions. This report examines housing adequacy and affordability, focusing on the physical condition of the state's housing stock and the financial burden placed on its residents.

Most quality measures indicate an improvement in housing conditions in New York State over the past 40 years. Figure 1 contains data on three common housing-quality measures collected in the Decennial Census by the U.S. Bureau of the Census—ownership rates, plumbing conditions, and crowding. All three measures reveal a steady improvement in the quality of New York State's housing.

Over the past forty years, the percentage of New Yorkers who own their own homes has steadily increased, from 30 percent in 1940 to over 49 percent today. Post 1980 data reveal a levelling off of the rapid increase in ownership rates of the 1970s, in part due to housing prices increasing faster than incomes.[14] At the national level, by 1987, ownership rates had declined to 64 percent from a 1980 rate of 65.6 percent. For younger households, the rate of ownership declined even more.[15]

New York trails the rest of the country in the percent of residents who own their home. The nearly 50/50 ownership-rental split statewide masks two different markets, one where the ownership rates conform to the national average, the other where they do not. Figure 2 gives clear evidence of the uniqueness of the New York City housing market, where renters predominate. Home ownership rates are, on average, three times higher outside of New York City and in line with national numbers. Further confirmation of this pattern can be found in Figure 3, which provides an analysis of tenure data for each of ten New York State housing regions.[16]

The physical condition of the state's housing stock has improved during this time period through the upgrading of existing units, the addition of new high-quality units, and the abandonment and, in some cases, the replacement of the oldest, substandard stock. U.S. Census data show that only 2.3 percent of the occupied housing units in the state lack complete plumbing facilities, a reduction from the 1940 levels of over 15 percent (Figure 1b), but virtually unchanged from the 1970 levels. New York's housing stock has always had relatively good plumbing because of the type of housing built in areas of high urban density.

Not only has the quality of the state's housing stock improved, but New Yorkers now have far more space to enjoy their better quality housing. Measures of housing crowding, given in Figure 1c, show that

NYS and US Housing Characteristics

1940 to 1980

From: Census of Housing

Percent Owner-Occupied Housing Units: 1940 to 1980

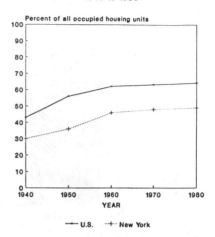

FIGURE 1A

Percent of Occupied Housing Units Lacking Complete Plumbing Facilities

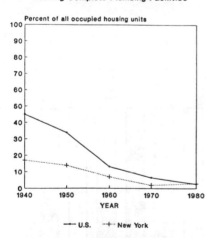

FIGURE 1B

Persons per Room 1940 to 1980

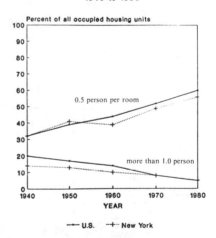

FIGURE 1C

fewer than five percent of the occupied units average more than one occupant per room. If anything, New Yorkers are increasingly finding ample room to roam. Since 1960, the percent of units with two or more rooms per person has expanded greatly.

FIGURE 2

Tenure Status of Housing Stock

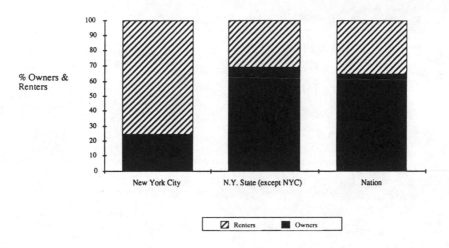

FIGURE 3

Tenure Status of Housing Stock by Region (1980)

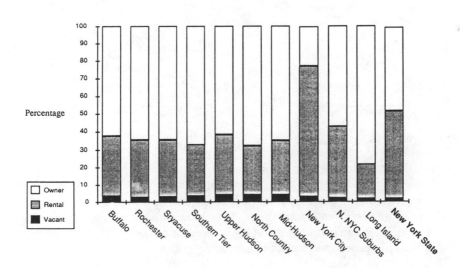

Although these numbers paint a relatively rosy picture of existing state housing conditions, they mask some very important problems. The generally excellent condition of the housing stock is not uniform across the state, nor are all state residents equally well housed. Further, our expectations about housing quality are constantly being upgraded while the housing stock is depreciating.[17]

To explore these issues fully, we examine New York State's housing conditions using a typology based on population density. This provides a useful way of organizing the heterogeneity in the state's housing markets and can serve as a basis for useful policy guidance. Statewide averages can mask significant differences between town and country, city and suburb, renters and owners.

The first population density grouping consists of households living in central cities outside of New York City. This category includes the next 12 most populous cities in the state and accounts for approximately seven percent of the state's housing units. These households share similarities not shared by the rural or New York City groupings. The second category includes the suburban households of non-central city portions of the state's standard Metropolitan Statistical Areas (SMSA's). This is the second largest grouping, totalling 39 percent of the households, and includes Long Island and Westchester County. Single family homeowners are the predominant housing/household type. A third group consists of units located in rural areas. These units fall outside of SMSA's and account for nine percent of the State's households. Three-quarters of these units are in the North Country or Southern Tier. The final group, New York City, accounts for 44 percent of the households in this study. The predominance of renter households living in multifamily dwellings sets it apart from the rest of the state.

Table 3 summarizes a number of housing quality characteristics for all New York State households, distinguishing location by urban density.[18] The final column of the table contains the statewide averages. In Tables 4 and 5 the same analysis is presented, distinguishing between renter and owner households. The first row of Table 3 contains a measure of the financial well-being of New York State households. Overall, 24 percent of the state's households have income less than 150 percent of the poverty line.[19] The table shows central city residents to be poorer than any other grouping. A comparison between Tables 4 and 5 shows that renters are poorer than owners, a finding consistent with the national pattern.[20]

These tables also examine regional differences in housing quality. Unfortunately, there are no universally accepted standards of housing quality—all measures are somewhat arbitrary. By developing our own

TABLE 3

**HOUSING AND HOUSEHOLD CHARACTERISTICS
OF ALL NYS HOUSEHOLDS BY URBAN DENSITY (1980)**

	NON-NYC CENTRAL CITY	SUBURBS	RURAL	NYC	STATE
% BELOW 150% OF POVERTY LINE	31.1%	14.6%	27.0%	30.6%	24.0%
% INADEQUATE	14.4	7.3	20.1	8.6	9.6
% CROWDED	2.0	2.2	2.3	7.6	4.6
% EXCESSIVE COST*	23.5	15.4	17.4	27.0	21.3

*Excessive cost exceeds 30% of household income for renters, 40% of household income for homeowners.
SOURCE: Calculated using the Public Use Microdata Sample from the 1980 Census of Housing.

TABLE 4

**HOUSING AND HOUSEHOLD CHARACTERISTICS
OF NYS RENTER HOUSEHOLDS BY URBAN DENSITY (1980)**

	NON-NYC CENTRAL CITY	SUBURBS	RURAL	NYC	STATE
% BELOW 150% OF POVERTY LINE	43.9%	28.1%	45.4%	36.0%	35.4%
% INADEQUATE	18.2	10.7	25.3	9.1	11.0
% CROWDED	2.2	4.0	3.3	8.9	7.0
% EXCESSIVE COST*	41.2	35.5	37.6	40.9	39.1

*Excessive cost exceeds 30% of household income for renters.
SOURCE: Calculated using the Public Use Microdata Sample from the 1980 Census of Housing.

measure (also somewhat arbitrary) we can compare housing quality across the state. Our measure combines the Census definitions of plumbing adequacy, whether the unit has central heating, and whether there is sole access to kitchen facilities. We categorize any unit lacking in any of these three measures as inadequate.[21] The inadequate proportion of the stock is

TABLE 5

**HOUSING AND HOUSEHOLD CHARACTERISTICS
OF NYS OWNER HOUSEHOLDS BY URBAN DENSITY (1980)**

	NON-NYC CENTRAL CITY	SUBURBS	RURAL	NYC	STATE
% BELOW 150% OF POVERTY LINE	16.0%	9.5%	19.5%	13.9%	12.2%
% INADEQUATE	9.9	6.1	17.9	7.0	8.1
% CROWDED	1.9	1.5	1.9	3.8	1.6
% EXCESSIVE COST*	11.2	11.6	11.3	15.9	12.1

*Excessive cost exceeds 40% of household income for owners.
SOURCE: Calculated using the Public Use Microdata Sample from the 1980 Census of Housing.

given in row 2 of Tables 3-5. As might be expected, we find renters living in less adequate units than owners. Statewide, 11 percent of renters live in inadequate housing as compared to only eight percent of owners. Adequacy problems are most common in the rural portions of the state. Rural structures are more likely to be lacking central heating than either plumbing or kitchen facilities.

Although only a small percentage of the state's residents are poorly housed, the absolute number of these households is substantial: 285,000 households live in crowded conditions, and over half a million households live in inadequate structures. Crowding is essentially a New York City phenomenon, accounting for over 75 percent of New York State's crowded units. This reflects the predominance of rental units, relatively high rents, and lower household income, all of which lead city residents to conserve on household space. Suburban renters are more likely to live in crowded households than other non-NYC residents, although the incidence of crowding is below four percent for this group.

Of further concern, housing quality problems affect different groups of New Yorkers differently. Figures 4 through 6 present data on housing quality and cost by poverty status. Quality problems are particularly severe for low-income groups. Analysis of the 1980 PUMS data shows that the incidence of crowding and inadequate housing is highly income conditioned. Low-income households (less than 150 percent of poverty line) are twice as likely (14 percent) to live in poor-quality housing than are wealthier households (seven percent). Not surprisingly, poor homeowners

FIGURE 4

Housing Quality By Poverty Status: N.Y.S. Renters (1980)

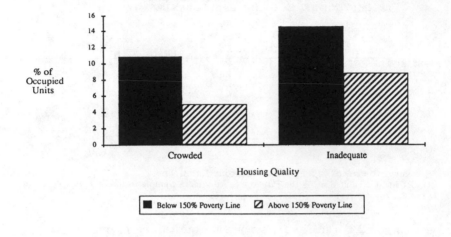

FIGURE 5

Housing Quality By Poverty Status: N.Y.S. Owners (1980)

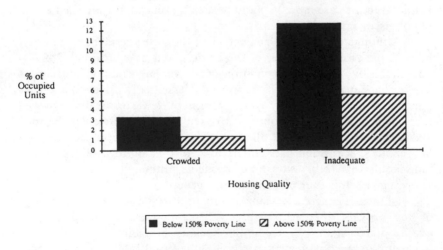

are most likely to reside in inadequate dwellings. Poor households are also three times more likely to live in crowded conditions.

Not only do poorer households consume poorer quality housing, but housing costs absorb higher portions of their more limited budgets. Over

FIGURE 6

Housing Affordability By Poverty Status and Tenure
(1980)

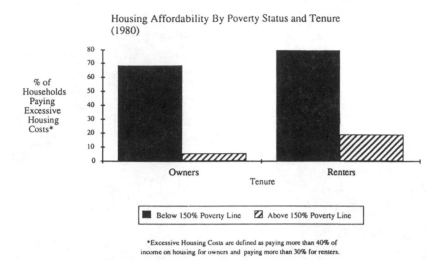

*Excessive Housing Costs are defined as paying more than 40% of
income on housing for owners and paying more than 30% for renters.

two-thirds of poor and near-poor households spend more than 40 percent of their income on housing, while less than six percent of wealthier households bear as high a burden. For renters, nearly 80 percent of those below 150 percent of the poverty line face housing costs that exceed the federal standard of 30 percent of household income. Overall, 39 percent of all renters face housing costs this high. Although, on average, renters are poorer than owners, nearly 20 percent of non-poor owners still face excessive housing costs.

In Figures 7 through 9 we use a different format to present housing quality data for all state households, all renters, and all homeowners. These Venn diagrams demonstrate the degree of multiple housing problems for different groups of New Yorkers, focusing on the income status of households, the adequacy of their housing choices, and the level of their housing costs. The outer square in Figures 7 through 9 represents the number of households in the analysis: either all households in New York State, just renter households, or just owners, respectively. The number of households below 150 percent of the poverty line, the number of owner households who pay more than 40 percent of their income in housing costs, the number of renter households who pay more than 30 percent of their income in housing costs, and the number of households suffering from at least one measure of inadequate housing are represented by the size of each of the three circles in the figure. The size of these circles is

FIGURE 7

New York State Household Characteristics:
Poverty Level, Excessive Costs and Inadequate
Housing (1980); All State Households.

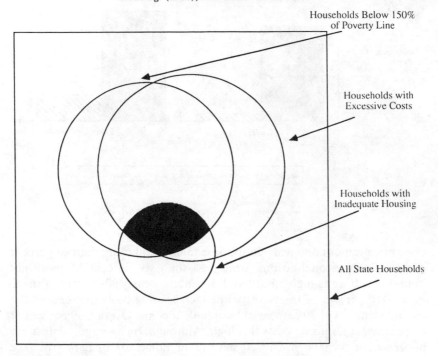

Legend:	
Characteristics	# of Households
All State Households in Sample	5,342,700
Below 150% of Poverty Line	1,347,700
Excessive Costs	1,512,200
Inadequate Housing	485,700
Below 150% Poverty & Excessive Costs	1,028,300
Below 150% Poverty & Inadequate Housing	192,900
Excessive Costs & Inadequate Housing	177,200
Below 150% Poverty & Excessive Costs & Inadequate Housing	141,100

proportional to the number of households in each category. Households
that are impacted by all three distress measures are portrayed by the
shaded portion in the figures. There are over 141,000 households in New

FIGURE 8

**New York State Household Characteristics:
Poverty Level, Excessive Costs and Inadequate
Housing (1980); All Renters.**

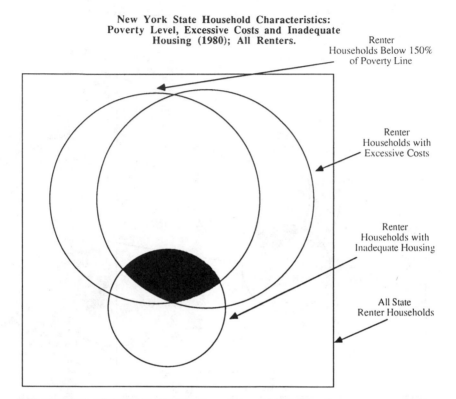

Renter
Households Below 150%
of Poverty Line

Renter
Households with
Excessive Costs

Renter
Households with
Inadequate Housing

All State
Renter Households

Legend:	
Characteristics	# of Households
All Renter Households in Sample	3,200,800
Below 150% of Poverty Line	1,134,100
Excessive Costs	1,252,100
Inadequate Housing	350,600
Below 150% Poverty & Excessive Costs	880,500
Below 150% Poverty & Inadequate Housing	165,800
Excessive Costs & Inadequate Housing	155,900
Below 150% Poverty & Excessive Costs & Inadequate Housing	126,400

York State that face all of these problems, 75,100 of which are renters
living in New York City.

A comparison of Figures 8 and 9 makes it clear that problems are

FIGURE 9

New York State Household Characteristics:
Poverty Level, Excessive Costs and Inadequate
Housing (1980); All Owners.

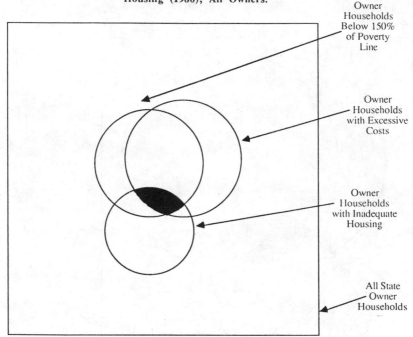

Owner
Households
Below 150%
of Poverty
Line

Owner
Households
with Excessive
Costs

Owner
Households
with Inadequate
Housing

All State
Owner
Households

Legend:	
Characteristics	# of Households
All Owner Households in Sample	2,141,900
Below 150% of Poverty Line	213,600
Excessive Costs	259,900
Inadequate Housing	135,100
Below 150% Poverty & Excessive Costs	147,800
Below 150% Poverty & Inadequate Housing	27,100
Excessive Costs & Inadequate Housing	21,000
Below 150% Poverty & Excessive Costs & Inadequate Housing	14,700

particularly severe for renters. Over 51 percent of New York State renters
fall somewhere within the circles, indicating some form of income or
housing distress, although only four percent of all renters fall in the shaded

portion representing the most severely impacted households. In contrast, just 20 percent of the state's homeowners fall into any of the impact categories and .7 percent fall into the multiple impact category.

A significant portion of households in New York State are faced with high rent-to-income ratios. These high rent-to-income ratios are especially typical of lower income New Yorkers. Over 1.25 million renter households pay more than 30 percent of their income on housing, representing nearly 40 percent of the state's renter households. Importantly, the vast majority (70 percent) of these households are low income, although not all are poorly housed. Only 18 percent of non-poor renter households (households whose family income exceeds 150 percent of the poverty line) elect to spend over 30 percent of their income on housing. For the most part, the decision to assume high rent burdens leads to adequate housing. Over five times as many poor and near poor renter households suffer excessive housing costs than live in inadequate housing.

The statewide patterns evidenced in these figures are replicated within each of the population density definitions created for this analysis. As an example, we note that the relationship between poverty and high rent-to-income ratios holds true in each of the density categories. In central cities 90 percent of the poor pay more than 40 percent of their income in rent—in rural areas 80 percent face the same high rent burdens. We find that central city residents are the most likely to exceed the 40 percent threshold—30 percent of these residents face rental cost burdens at least this high. Suburban residents are far less likely to pay such a large percentage of their income in rent—only 24 percent do so. This undoubtedly reflects the relative affluence of suburban jurisdictions where only 15 percent of the renters are below the near-poverty line (as opposed to 27 percent in central cities).

Substantial differences in housing consumption patterns are also found for different racial groups in New York State (Table 6). In general, black households face more housing-related problems than whites. Blacks are more likely to live in crowded conditions, occupy substandard housing, and pay larger portions of their more limited income on housing.

To a large extent these differences reflect higher white household income. Fully 40 percent of black households are within 150 percent of the poverty line, while less than 20 percent of whites are as poor.[22] However, as can be seen in Table 7, income differentials do not explain the entire pattern. When we compare black and white housing choices for similar income groupings, we still find black households to be relatively disadvantaged. For instance, 12.5 percent of near-poor blacks live in inadequate housing costing above the 30 percent of household income threshold, while

TABLE 6

**HOUSING AND HOUSEHOLD CHARACTERISTICS
NYS HOUSEHOLDS BY RACE (1980)**

	BLACK	WHITE
% BELOW 150% POVERTY LINE	40.4%	19.8%
% OWNER OCCUPIED	23.1	55.7
% INADEQUATE	13.0	8.7
% CROWDED	10.1	2.7
% EXCESSIVE COST	37.9	20.8
% POOR & EXCESSIVE COST	29.6	13.2
% INADEQUATE & EXCESSIVE COST	6.2	2.1
% POOR, CROWDED, INADEQUATE & EXCESSIVE COST	0.7	0.1

SOURCE: US Department of Census PUMS DATA (1980)

TABLE 7

**HOUSING AND HOUSEHOLD CHARACTERISTICS
NYS HOUSEHOLDS BY RACE (1980)**

	BLACK		WHITE	
	Below 150% Poverty	Over 150% Poverty	Below 150% Poverty	Over 150% Poverty
% OWNER OCCUPIED	9.8%	32.0%	33.0%	61.4%
% INADEQUATE	16.1	10.9	14.2	7.3
% CROWDED	14.4	7.2	5.3	2.1
% EXCESSIVE COST	73.3	13.9	66.3	9.6
% INADEQUATE & EXCESSIVE COST	12.5	2.0	8.2	0.6
% CROWDED, INADEQUATE & EXCESSIVE COST	1.9	0.0	0.5	0.0

SOURCE: US Department of Census PUMS DATA (1980)

only eight percent of similarly situated white households spend as much of their income on housing. Differences in ownership patterns are even more striking. Over 60 percent of non-poor white households own their own homes, nearly double the comparable ownership rate for black households.[23]

These differences can be seen visually in the Venn Diagrams presented in Figures 10 through 12. These figures allow further comparison of housing-related distress by race and occupancy status. The housing and income differentials facing whites and non-whites are striking. While two-thirds of white households suffer no distress on our measures, only 42 percent of non-white households are as fortunate. Similarly, non-white households are more than three times more likely than white households to suffer from all three measures of housing-related stress (5.6 percent to 1.8 percent). The problem is most severe for renters. The combination of being both non-white and renting leaves a household particularly vulnerable to housing-related problems. 61 percent of this group suffer some housing or income-related stress, and over six percent suffer from all three problems.

To some extent these findings reflect historical patterns of location and differing choices over family structure and housing type. Large families of all types are more likely to live in crowded conditions in New York City, which historically has been a residential center for blacks in New York State. But more importantly, these findings may reflect the existence of discrimination (past and present) in housing markets that limit the choices of minority households.

Finally, we examine housing quality as a function of the age of the housing stock. Although the relationship between the age of a housing unit and its quality is ambiguous, older units generally require greater maintenance. This creates a problem when wealthier households upgrade their housing choices in newer structures, leaving the older stock to those less able to maintain it. Twelve percent of the housing stock built before 1939 suffers from at least one of the conditions that would classify it as inadequate, nearly twice the inadequacy rate of the remainder of the housing stock.

This pattern will be increasingly important as we move toward the next century. In 1980, 43 percent of the state's housing stock was over 40 years old. In New York City, the problem is potentially more severe; nearly 50 percent of the housing was built before 1939, and another 16 percent was built before 1949. Unless these structures receive sufficient maintenance, they will eventually be added to the stock of substandard housing. The rate that buildings deteriorate depends upon the economic calcula-

FIGURE 10

New York State Household Characteristics by Race:
Poverty Level, Excessive Costs and Inadequate
Housing (1980); All State Households.

All State White HouseHolds

Non-white Households

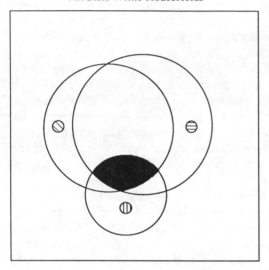

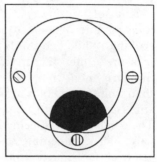

⊘ Households Below 150%
    of Poverty Line

⊜ Households with
    Excessive Costs

⊕ Households with
    Inadequate Housing

Legend:		
Characteristics	White Households	Non-white Households
All State Households in Sample	4,290,700	1,052,000
Below 150% of Poverty Line	877,900	469,800
Excessive Costs	1,059,600	452,400
Inadequate Housing	348,100	137,600
Below 150% Poverty & Excessive Costs	665,100	363,200
Below 150% Poverty & Inadequate Housing	118,900	74,000
Excessive Costs & Inadequate Housing	105,500	71,700
Below 150% Poverty & Excessive Costs & Inadequate Housing	81,500	59,600

tions of their owners. Public policies can have an important influence on
these investment decisions.

To sum up, housing quality problems in New York State are far less
pervasive than problems of housing affordability. Quality problems differ

FIGURE 11

New York State Renter Household Characteristics by Race:
Poverty Level, Excessive Costs and Inadequate
Housing (1980); All Renters Households.

All State White Households   Non-white Households

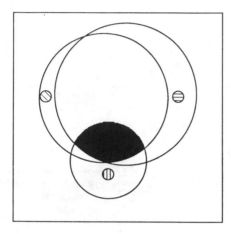

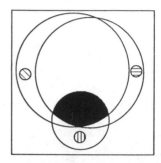

Legend:		
		Non-white
Characteristics	White Households	Households
All Renter Households in Sample	2,273,400	927,400
Below 150% of Poverty Line	682,800	451,300
Excessive Costs	825,700	421,400
Inadequate Housing	228,300	122,300
Below 150% Poverty & Excessive Costs	532,000	348,500
Below 150% Poverty & Inadequate Housing	95,400	70,400
Excessive Costs & Inadequate Housing	88,900	67,000
Below 150% Poverty & Excessive Costs & Inadequate Housing	69,700	56,800

depending upon the ownership status of the occupant, the race and income
of the household, and the location of the housing unit. After decades of
continuous housing-quality improvements, what quality problems remain
are found in the older housing stock, primarily rented and located in

FIGURE 12

New York State Household Characteristics by Race:
Poverty Level, Excessive Costs and Inadequate
Housing (1980); All Owner Households.

All State White Households

Non-white Households

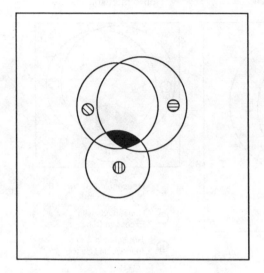

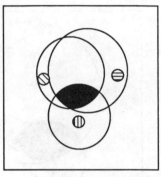

⊘ Households Below 150%
    of Poverty Line

⊖ Households with
    Inadequate Housing

⦀ Households with
    Excessive Costs

Legend:		
Characteristics	White Households	Non-White Households
All Owner Households in Sample	2,017,300	124,600
Below 150% of Poverty Line	195,100	18,500
Excessive Costs	233,900	26,000
Inadequate Housing	119,800	15,300
Below 150% Poverty & Excessive Costs	133,100	14,700
Below 150% Poverty & Inadequate Housing	23,500	3,600
Excessive Costs & Inadequate Housing	16,600	4,700
Below 150% Poverty & Excessive Costs & Inadequate Housing	11,900	2,800

central city locations. Households living in inadequate housing are more likely to be black and poor. Although the rural housing stock is much more likely to be substandard, there are too few units in these areas of the state to have a major impact on the statewide aggregates.

4

The Special Problem of Affordability

The evidence is quite clear—American households' major housing problem is affordability.[24] Over time, the physical condition of the housing stock has gradually improved to the point where only a small percentage of occupied structures fail to meet generally accepted housing quality standards (which is not to dismiss the job as done). However, improvements in housing conditions have been at the expense of increased financial burdens facing renters and homeowners.

In today's housing market, the price of newly constructed housing outstrips the financial resources of most New Yorkers. Even the cost of existing housing has become prohibitively expensive. As a result, home ownership is an unreachable dream for many. This phenomenon is not limited to New York City alone. Communities throughout the state have experienced rapidly rising prices. Albany, where housing dollars once stretched far, has become one of the most rapidly appreciating housing markets in the country. In some areas of the state only the comparatively wealthy can afford to enter the local housing market.

Rapidly rising house values and increases in contract rents have led housing analysts, as well as mortgage lenders, to readjust their guidelines for determining acceptable housing cost burdens. At one time, analysts considered the allocation of one weekly pay check per month to be an acceptable level of housing expenditures. Today, we find over half of the state's renters paying more than 25 percent of their household income on rent. The Department of Housing and Urban Development has revised its guidelines, establishing an allocation of 30 percent of income as acceptable for renters and 40 percent for owners. In fact, over one-fifth of the state's renters devote more than 50 percent of their income to housing costs.

The statewide figures in this study are based on the 1980 Census of Housing. More recent data for selective areas within New York State indicate that housing affordability problems are every bit as severe today as in 1980. Although the affordability index constructed by the National Association of Realtors indicates that housing was more affordable in

1985 than in 1980, because of the sharp decline in home mortgage interest rates, the steep increase in housing prices in New York State may have more than countered this effect.[25] Further, the affordability index may not reflect the housing cost burdens faced by families too poor to purchase the median priced home or those who live in rental housing.

The 1983 Annual Housing Survey for the New York City Metropolitan area shows this problem clearly. In 1980, the housing cost-to-income ratios exceeded 40 percent for 12.1 percent of homeowners. In the 1983 survey, this percentage rose to 12.7%. Housing cost burdens for renters have also increased. In 1980, 35.4 percent of metropolitan area renter households paid more than 35 percent of their income for rent. By 1983 the corresponding percentage had increased to 38.2 percent.[26] There has been no evidence to indicate this trend has reversed since 1983.

Within New York City affordability problems are even more severe, despite attempts to control housing costs through regulation of the rental market. Poor New Yorkers are especially vulnerable. The price of land in New York City, combined with the cost of new construction, makes it virtually impossible to construct unsubsidized units at anything but the top end of the market.[27] Compounding this problem, or perhaps a reflection of it, are the extremely low vacancy rates. For most low-income tenants, there is virtually no affordable housing available in New York City. In part, this shortage of affordable housing explains the plight of the homeless, yet this is just the tip of the affordable housing iceberg. (Note, however, that the vast majority of the poor are housed.)

In general, housing cost burdens fall as incomes rise. Thus, poor households pay a larger percentage of their income for housing than wealthier households. This problem is exacerbated by the poor's limited resource base. Consider a poor family with $6,000 in income, paying 50 percent of their income in rent (if they can find an apartment to rent for $250 per month). This leaves only $250 per month for the rest of their budget—not nearly enough to pay for life's other necessities. Affordability problems of this magnitude are common for the poor, not only in New York City, but across the entire state.

To develop a measure of the availability of affordable housing in New York State, the PUMS data is used to compare the number of potentially affordable units with the number of low-income households.[28] Based on HUD standards, a housing unit is defined to be affordable if it rents at 30 percent of the household's income. This is not to say that every household must choose to live in a unit renting at the HUD standard. Rather, we seek to develop a sense of the balance between potential demand and supply.

Table 8 presents data on the number of low-income households found in ten income groupings. For each grouping, we calculate the number of units in New York State with contract rents no greater than 30 percent of the midpoint of the corresponding income class, net of units affordable to lower income groupings. Thus, the number of units affordable to the poorest decile is 27,300. An additional 9,200 units would be defined as affordable to the next income decile, but considered too expensive, by this measure, for the poorest grouping (column 3).

Table 8 reveals that there were far fewer affordable units than households with incomes below $4000 in 1980. Only 36 percent of these households could have found housing renting at 30 percent of their income. In fact, far fewer than 36 percent of these households lived in

TABLE 8

NEW YORK STATE'S AFFORDABLE HOUSING GAP

INCOME LEVEL (1980$)	# HOUSEHOLDS	AFFORDABLE UNITS*	PERCENT COVERAGE**
0 - $ 999	122,800	27,300	22%
1000 - 1999	54,700	9,200	17
2000 - 2999	112,400	70,100	62
3000 - 3999	170,800	59,400	35
4000 - 4999	70,500	146,500	>100
5000 - 5999	44,100	150,800	>100
6000 - 6999	27,700	248,700	>100
7000 - 7999	20,200	250,500	>100
8000 - 8999	11,900	303,400	>100
9000 - 9999	7,500	313,700	>100

*Affordable units are defined as those units renting at 30% of household income in each respective income grouping.
**% Coverage defined as the number of affordable units divided by the number of low-income households in category.
Calculated from PUMS data.

affordable units because some higher income households chose to live in
lower cost housing. For those households with income exceeding $4000,
the potential number of available, affordable units exceeds the number of
households (Figure 13), although some of these units are undoubtedly
rented by lower income households.

FIGURE 13

New York State's Affordable Housing Gap

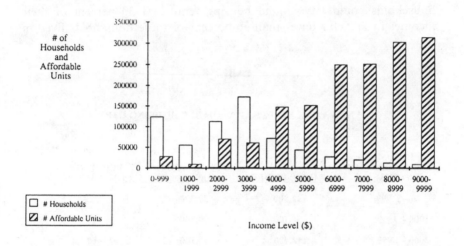

Although there is an aggregate shortage of affordable rental units for
low-income households in New York State, there are substantial regional
variations. Table 9 examines the balance of affordable housing units and
low-income households in each New York State region. This table focuses
on households with income below $6,000, accounting for 86 percent of the
households below the poverty line.[29] While some higher income households also face affordability problems, the crunch is most severe for those
below the poverty line.

Statewide, the number of low-income households exceeds the
number of affordable units by 25 percent. However, there are marked
differences between the supply and demand for low-income, affordable
units across regions. The supply shortage appears to be most severe in the
New York metropolitan area. On Long Island, there are only one-half as
many units renting at affordable rents as there are needy households.
Relatively few low-income families live in this region (only 19,000 by our

TABLE 9

SUPPLY AND DEMAND CHARACTERISTICS FOR AFFORDABLE HOUSING
BY NEW YORK STATE REGION (1980)

REGION	# AFFORDABLE UNITS*	# LOW INCOME HOUSEHOLDS**	%COVERAGE UNITS/HOUSEHOLDS
BUFFALO	28,700	30,5001	94%
ROCHESTER	16,000	17,800	90
SYRACUSE	24,100	27,000	89
SOUTHERN TIER	24,500	21,500	114
UPPER HUDSON	22,400	17,400	129
NORTH COUNTRY	14,300	9,200	155
MID HUDSON	9,700	12,800	76
NEW YORK CITY	301,000	407,300	74
NORTH NYC SUBURBS	13,800	17,000	78
LONG ISLAND	8,800	19,000	46
TOTAL	463,300	579,500	80%

*Affordable units are defined as those units renting at $1800 per year or less (30% of household income of $6000).
**Households with less than $6,000 income (see text for more details).

estimates), so the problem in absolute terms is less severe than in other parts of the state. New York City, on the other hand, is desperately short of affordable housing. The number of low-income households seeking affordable shelter exceeds the available supply by one-third, or by over 100,000 households. This exceeds ten times the shortfall of any other region.

Not every region lacks sufficient affordable housing. The Buffalo and Rochester regions have nearly equal numbers of households and units. In Syracuse, affordable supply falls short of low-income demand by almost 3000 units. Interestingly, in 1980 the North Country had many more units renting at affordable rates than there were low-income families to fill them. As a result, low-cost units are filled with wealthier households who bear relatively low housing cost burdens.

Although the situation in the North Country seems to indicate little cause of concern, we must be cautious interpreting this data. First, in Table 9, the matching between households and affordable units is made irrespective of household size. If poorer households are larger and cheaper units are smaller, our matching procedure would understate the degree of housing distress for low-income households. This will be true across all regions. Additional research could profitably explore the housing quality/ size dimension of the affordability issue.

Second, even though Table 9 indicates that some regions face shortages of affordable housing and others have such housing in ample supply, sub-regional housing markets may differ from the regional picture. For example, the North Country is far too large a geographic unit for all conditions to be the same. Ample supply of affordable housing in the most rural portion of this region may have little impact on the poor household looking for housing in the Fort Drum area.[30] Similarly, housing market conditions are likely to vary across metropolitan areas.

Third, these totals are not adjusted for housing quality. Many of the state's affordable units are vacant and inadequate. Nearly 21 percent of the vacant units are inadequate under our definition and remain vacant, undoubtedly, because they offer such a poor housing choice. In the North Country region the problem is more intense; 32 percent of the affordable rental units are inadequate. Inadequate units are usually the last to be rented. For example, in the Buffalo region, 26 percent of the vacant, affordable, rental units are inadequate.[31] It is unlikely that the vacant stock will be a useful source of many additional affordable units without significant rehabilitation.

How Large is the Housing Cost Gap?

Low-income households face a shortage of affordable housing, although the magnitude of the problem declines as household income increases. This section makes use of the 1980 PUMS data to estimate the aggregate size of the gap between household income and the cost of adequate housing in New York State.

It is one matter to claim that there is a shortage of affordable housing in New York State. It is quite another to analyze what the cost of ending this shortage would be. One approach is to construct new housing or rehabilitate existing housing that would be used for low-income households. Table 9 provides estimates of the number of affordable units required to house the poor. Another approach is to calculate the dollar cost of a subsidy program that would make existing housing affordable for low-income households. These estimates can then be used by policy makers seeking to evaluate the potential impact of a housing subsidy program.

For this analysis, the rental cost gap is defined to be equal to the difference between the cost of renting a moderate-quality apartment and 30 percent of the household income of low-income households (the official poor and those near poor, i.e., below 150 percent of the poverty line). This definition provides a conservative estimate of the housing cost gap. If households were expected to assume a larger percentage of their housing costs, or if public policies provided access to higher quality units, estimates of the rental cost gap would be correspondingly larger.

Table 10 presents an analysis of the rental cost gap for each of New York State's housing regions in 1980, the last year that Census data are available. Median rents (1980 dollars) ranged from $2,300 per year in the North Country to $4,200 per year ($350 per month) on Long Island. Household incomes required to rent the median rental unit at 30 percent of income ranged from $7,700 to $14,000 (column 3).

Families with zero household income face the maximum possible cost gap, equivalent to the median annual rent in the region. The gap declines as household income increases and reaches zero when 30 percent of household income is sufficient to rent the median-valued apartment. The average cost gap is given in column 5. The size of the gap generally increases across regions as median rents increase, although there are some exceptions. For instance, in the Upper Hudson region, average gaps are higher than in the Syracuse region, but housing costs are cheaper, reflecting the relatively lower tenant incomes in the area.

This analysis reveals that it would require an increase in household income of $1.8 billion annually (1980 dollars) to close the rental cost gap.[32] Some may argue that calculating a housing cost gap based on the median-valued rental unit in the region overstates the problem of low household incomes. After all, half of the occupied rental units in the state have contract rents below this level. In Table 11, we recalculate the gap based on the unit renting at the 25th percentile of the distribution. This reduces the aggregate size of the gap to $1.1 billion annually (1980 dollars) because more households are able to afford this standard of housing, and the average gap size will be smaller for each qualifying household.

A comparison between the first column of Tables 10 and 11 reveals that median-level rents exceed 25th percentile rents by a range of $47 per month in the Buffalo area to $72 per month in the northern New York City suburbs. Lower rents will result in smaller average cost gaps and are the main explanation for why the aggregate annual gap for the 25th percentile

TABLE 10

HOUSING COST GAP FOR RENTERS (MEDIAN QUALITY UNIT)
(1980 DOLLARS)

REGION	ANNUAL MEDIAN RENT	INCOME NEEDED (30% RULE)	% LOW INCOME HOUSEHOLDS WITH GAP	AVERAGE GAP	TOTAL GAP
BUFFALO	$2,544	$8,480	33.9%	$1,424	$76,041,600
ROCHESTER	2,904	9,680	29.2	1,685	55,942,000
SYRACUSE	2,544	8,480	34.4	1,366	58,874,600
SOUTHERN TIER	2,448	8,160	36.6	1,269	52,663,500
UPPER HUDSON	2,478	8,260	29.9	1,381	47,368,300
NORTH COUNTRY	2,310	7,700	37.4	1,085	22,134,000
MID HUDSON	3,144	10,480	32.9	1,883	48,769,700
NEW YORK CITY	2,988	9,960	32.9	1,817	1,264,450,300
NORTH NYC SUBURBS	3,684	12,280	21.9	2,369	88,126,800
LONG ISLAND	4,200	14,000	25.7	2,788	114,029,200

$1,828,400,000

*Housing cost gap defined as difference between 30% of household income and 30% of income required to rent median rental unit in region. Low income households have income less than 150% of poverty line.
Calculated from 1980 PUMS data.

valued unit is approximately $700,000,000 smaller than one based on the median unit. In either case, the gap between the household income of the poor and the cost of adequate housing is appreciable.

An alternative measure of the housing cost gap is to compare the financial capacity of renters to the costs of owning a home. Home ownership has long been considered part of the American dream, and policy makers have identified home ownership as a desirable housing goal. Of course, not all renters care to assume the responsibilities of home ownership. Nor is universal home ownership necessarily a preferred policy option. Rather, we provide these numbers as an alternative estimate of the size of the housing affordability problem.[33]

TABLE 11

HOUSING COST GAP FOR RENTERS (25TH PCT. QUALITY)
(1980 DOLLARS)

REGION	ANNUAL 25th Pct RENT	INCOME NEEDED (30% RULE)	% LOW INCOME HOUSEHOLDS WITH GAP	AVERAGE GAP	TOTAL GAP
BUFFALO	$1,980	$6600	31.2%	$ 950	$46,740,000
ROCHESTER	2,220	7400	27.3	1,094	33,914,000
SYRACUSE	1,896	6320	30.5	845	32,279,000
SOUTHERN TIER	1,860	6200	32.0	822	29,756,400
UPPER HUDSON	1,947	6610	31.6	960	30,528,000
NORTH COUNTRY	1,683	5610	28.4	694	10,757,000
MID HUDSON	2,382	7940	29.8	1,281	30,103,500
NYC	2,220	7400	30.2	1,173	749,429,700
NORTH NYC SUBURBS	2,820	9400	20.7	1,619	56,826,900
LONG ISLAND	3,420	11400	24.7	2,104	82,687,200

$1,103,021,700

*Housing cost gap defined as difference between 30% of household income and 30% of income required to rent median rental unit in region. Low income households have income less than 150% of poverty line.
Calculated from 1980 PUMS data.

The ownership cost gap, based on HUD guidelines, equals the difference between 40 percent of household income and the annual carrying costs of a home at the 25th percentile housing value.[34] Thus, three-fourths of the homes within the region are more expensive than the target property. This analysis assumes the ownership gap is restricted to renters under the age of 65, the group most likely to pursue ownership options.

Table 12 presents this analysis for each of the ten state regions. The table contains the 1980 value of the house in the 25th percentile; the income needed to carry the property taxes, mortgage payments, and insurance on the home; the percentage of renters under the age of 65 who would be

Housing New York

TABLE 12

HOUSING COST GAP FOR HOME OWNERSHIP* (1980$)

REGION	25% HOUSING VALUE	INCOME NEEDED (40% RULE)	% OF RENTERS WITH OWNERSHIP GAP	AVERAGE GAP	TOTAL GAP
BUFFALO	$28,750	$8,970	36.2%	$1,800	$81,360,000
ROCHESTER	32,500	10,140	37.5	1,861	63,646,200
SYRACUSE	26,250	8,190	34.4	1,497	51,646,500
SOUTHERN TIER	23,750	7,410	33.4	1,362	41,677,200
UPPER HUDSON	28,750	8,970	32.5	1,782	50,252,400
NORTH COUNTRY	21,250	6,630	27.4	1,137	13,530,360
MID HUDSON	32,500	10,140	39.5	1,789	44,546,100
NEW YORK CITY	42,500	13,260	51.6	2,659	2,285,942,300
NORTH NYC SUBURBS	57,500	17,940	51.6	3,337	230,586,700
LONG ISLAND	42,500	13,260	40.0	2,355	125,286,000

$2,988,473,700

*Housing cost gap defined as difference between 40% of household income and 40% of income required to carry 90% mortgage on housing unit of 25th percentile value in region. Calculated from 1980 PUMS data.

unable to cover these payments if they allocated 40 percent of their income to housing; and the average and total size of the ownership gap. Average cost gaps range from $1,137 in the North Country to $3,337 in the northern New York City suburbs.

On the basis of our sample evidence, over one million renter households with household heads younger than 65 have insufficient income to cover the carrying cost of a home valued at the 25th percentile within the region. The total estimated annual owner housing cost gap is estimated to be approximately $3.0 billion (1980 dollars). This is a conservative estimate in that it seeks to achieve a modest level of housing services (25th percentile home), it has a relatively high-income requirement, and it assumes that the ten percent downpayment and closing fees are available to the recipient. This last assumption is obviously unrealistic. Adding in the downpayment and typical closing costs on these purchases increases the annual owner cost gap by a one-time payment of approximately $4,000 per household for a total of nearly $4.8 billion. In any event, providing renters the resources to purchase housing would be twice as expensive as closing the renter cost gap.

The ability of New York State renters to purchase adequate housing falls far short of the cost of this housing. The housing cost gap is estimated to range from $1 billion to $3 billion annually (1980 dollars), far larger than current state expenditures on housing. This gap between the ability of households to consume housing services and the cost of those services forms the major housing policy dilemma facing New York State today.

How policy makers should handle this dilemma is unclear. Should the state subsidize lower cost housing or encourage households to move to lower cost regions? Should the state seek regulatory relief or encourage localities to hold down housing costs with more regulation? Should all households facing housing cost gaps be assisted, and to what extent? What forms should housing subsidies take? An examination of these questions will have to wait until chapter 7.

5

The Rent Regulated Market

No discussion about current housing conditions in New York State would be complete without an analysis of the impact of rent regulations on the New York City housing market. Virtually all rental units in New York City are subject to some form of regulation, as are rental units in 64 municipalities throughout the state. In this section, we take a close look at the genesis of rent regulations and their potential effects on the functioning of the housing market.

Rent control was first introduced in New York State in 1920. The current variant of this law dates to federal attempts to control war time prices, including housing costs, in 1943.[35] Since 1943, rent control laws have metamorphosed through a number of stages, moving in the direction of either tighter or looser controls, depending upon the political currents of the time. Recently, there have been increased levels of political conflict over the status of rent regulation.

Today, rent control and its close cousin, rent stabilization, directly influence the contract rent for over 1.2 million apartments in New York City, which represent over one-third of all New York State rental units. Indirectly, these regulations influence the rent of every unit in rent regulated jurisdictions because of the complex interactions between the controlled and decontrolled sectors.

The rent regulations system has evolved in an extremely complex and arcane form since its inception. Until 1969, rent control affected only those structures built prior to 1947. In that year the State Legislature enacted the Rent Stabilization Law in response to rapidly rising rents in structures built after the rent control laws were implemented. This law placed apartments of 6 or more units, built post-1947, under the rent stabilization laws. Rent stabilization was a milder form of control, created as a vehicle to provide financial relief to middle-income tenants living in newer buildings. At this point, rent-controlled apartments mostly housed lower income families.

Two major swings in the evolution of New York City's rent

regulations caused the distinction between controls and stabilization to disintegrate. In 1971, the Vacancy Decontrol Law freed rent controlled and stabilized apartments from rent regulations when voluntarily vacated by tenants, allowing building owners to increase rents to market levels. Market rents had climbed appreciably due to inflation, and the two-tier system resulted in large variations in the rental rates for comparable apartments, depending upon the rate of tenant turnover. This imbalance fanned the flames of tenant resistance and lead to the second major swing in control laws. Under the Emergency Tenant Protection Act of 1974, the Vacancy Decontrol Law was rescinded and voluntarily vacated apartments became subject to Rent Stabilization. As a result, there was a gradual blurring of the distinction of the control status of apartments that primarily served poor households and those that contained middle class constituencies. Today, 200,000 apartments are rent controlled and over 900,000 are rent stabilized. Eventually all controlled apartments will fall under the stabilization laws.

The existing rent regulation system is administratively complex, to say the least. The state is required to make numerous administrative findings to determine Maximum Base Rent (MBR) levels for various apartments as well as judgments concerning rights of occupancy. The New York State Department of Housing and Community Renewal (DHCR) must also determine the rate at which controlled apartments can approach established rent target goals. This requires detailed analyses of management and utility costs facing landlords, as well as certification of building improvements.

The state's ability to run the rent regulation program has recently come under legislative scrutiny. DHCR has received sharp criticism for its management of the system. Despite recent improvements, there is a deeper question as to whether any administrative agency can do an adequate job administering a system as complex as the one required to set housing costs for 1.2 million New York City apartments.[36]

All of these headaches have not come cheaply—close regulatory supervision is expensive. The New York State Budget Bureau estimates that $21 million of the DHCR budget is allocated to running the rent regulation system. These are direct budgeted costs and do not include the commitment of time and money by both landlords and tenants.

By now, rent regulation has become an accepted feature of the New York City housing market, despite the vigorous arguments for deregulation made by the Real Estate Board, other landlord organizations, and good government groups. Fears of voters' reprisals have kept elected officials from undertaking serious reform of the existing system. If anything, recent proposals and directives from the Governor's office indicate that rent regulations are likely to become more embracing. Proposals have been made to expand the domain of regulations, including establishing an inheritable right to a controlled apartment—something landlord groups are dead set against.

Despite the level of political support, housing economists are virtually unanimous in their opposition to rent regulations.[37] Rent controls are viewed as an extremely inefficient way to achieve redistribution from rich to poor and have deleterious long-term effects on housing markets. Even those few policy analysts who argue in support of controls do so unenthusiastically. They acknowledge that the protection rent controls offer the poor is achieved at a very high price, but they argue that the value of allowing the poor to maintain their apartments outweighs the costs.

Since it is rare that a policy can attract such widespread opposition in the analytic community, it is useful to review the arguments rent control critics make. Although not all of these arguments are indisputable, they form a sufficiently persuasive whole to merit serious consideration. By thinking about housing policy options for the next century, we can go beyond the current political debate. Given the extended time horizon, it may be possible to develop a set of policies that will protect today's tenants, but will also allow the housing market of the 21st century to operate less encumbered by rent regulations.

Critics of rent regulations focus on a number of major problems that rent regulations create. Two issues concern the impact of controls upon the suppliers of housing services. First, analysts claim that the existence of rent control has a chilling effect on new housing construction. Why should investors develop new housing if they are unable to realize the full value of their asset? Second, rent control leads to reduced maintenance of existing structures and a reduction in the rental stock through abandonment and conversion.

The first claim is difficult to validate because new, unsubsidized construction is not subject to rent control laws. Critics claim, however, that past capricious actions of government regulators, by imposing regulations where they previously did not exist, discourages new housing construction. At least twice in the past, New York City has regulated previously unregulated rents. In 1969, New York City changed the status of buildings constructed after 1947 by placing them under the rent stabilization laws. Later, structures built under the 421 tax subsidy program had their decontrolled status revoked. These actions provide ample evidence to confirm the suspicions of those owners who fear that all buildings may someday be subject to controls.

It is difficult to assess whether controls have a chilling effect upon building construction because the effect of expectations is difficult to isolate empirically. The recent building boom in Manhattan is partial evidence that the fear of post-construction regulation is not so chilling as to discourage all building, at least in times of high demand. How much more housing might be supplied today if no threat of controls existed is an unanswered question. Further, builders' expectations do not change easily. Even the end of controls may not be sufficient to restore confidence among housing developers. After all, the abolition of rent control cannot erase the memory of rent controls having been imposed on an unregulated market.

Rent regulations choke off the supply of rental housing in a second way. Regulations restrict collectable rental income and encourage some landlords to sell their buildings to tenants by turning them into co-ops, rather than continue to manage them as rental units. This reduces the supply of rental housing even further. Over the past decade, four percent of New York City's rental stock has been removed from the rental stock through the cooperative conversion process.[38]

Rent regulations can also have a negative impact on building maintenance. Unless landlords pass along maintenance costs by increasing rents, there is little reason to upgrade their buildings. Indeed, one way a landlord could increase his economic return is by underinvesting in housing services and letting maintenance decline.

There is little disagreement about the potentially detrimental effect rent regulations have upon the incentives of landlords to upgrade their buildings. The impact of these disincentives will depend on the motivations underlying landlord behavior and the competitiveness of the housing market. Even in a housing market where conditions are ripe for disinvestment, we would expect the impact of rent regulations on maintenance decisions to differ across landlords. Maintenance choices will differ depending upon the owner's plans for disposing of the building (e.g., abandonment or sale), neighborhood factors, and upon the characteristics and maintenance behavior of tenants.

Empirically, the evidence that rent controls lead to under-maintenance is more difficult to establish. The causes of housing deterioration and abandonment are far more complex than the existence of rent regulations alone. To further confound this issue, housing abandonment and deterioration have occurred in jurisdictions that never had controls. Further, in some of the most poorly maintained housing, rent regulations have not been the effective constraint on collectable rental income. These units are actually renting below the levels that rent regulation would allow.[39] In these cases, the income of the tenants living in these structures is too low to support higher rents, and rent payments are frequently delinquent or underpaid at existing levels.

It is not surprising that housing occupied by low-income tenants with insufficient rent-paying capacity is likely to become dilapidated, whether there is rent control or not. Not all rent controlled or stabilized buildings are undermaintained; however, rent regulations provide an additoinal reason for landlords to undermaintain building quality. When the costs of new construction far exceed the costs of maintaining the existing stock, rent control provides an incentive that moves the market in a socially undesirable direction.

The presence of rent regulations also influences the behavior of those who demand housing services. Critics charge that the opportunity to consume housing at below market rates leads consumers to overconsume housing. Renters choose to live in larger, higher quality housing than they otherwise would have chosen at competitive market prices. While "overconsumption" of housing services is a fringe benefit for those tenants lucky enough to possess a controlled apartment, it is socially inefficient. Potential tenants willing to pay higher rents are precluded from exercising their housing choices.

A further consequence of overconsumption is a tightening of the housing market. Proponents of rent control acknowledge that the low vacancy rate in New York City discourages renters from searching for a new apartment, even if that new apartment provided a closer match between housing consumption and preference.[40] This may mean some households end up consuming less housing than they would prefer in a market with more opportunities. Ironically, the mismatch between demand and supply is offered as precisely the reason that rent control is needed. They argue that any relaxation of rent regulations would only place those renters without options at the landlord's mercy.

The existing system makes tenants even less likely to move than the incentives outlined above suggest. Landlords are permitted greater increases in apartment rents when apartments are vacated. Thus, vacating a controlled apartment surely means facing the prospect of finding smaller quarters, at what is likely to be even higher rents. This discourages households from moving, even when their housing consumption falls far out of sync with their housing demand. In sum, rent regulations lead to the overconsumption of housing, which exacerbates the supply shortages created by the same regulations.

The protection of existing tenants and the creation of housing bargains explain the political popularity of rent regulations. However, the allocational effects induced by price controls are costly to other members of society. New migrants seeking to enter controlled housing markets, children reaching the age of independence, and young families who have outgrown their present space needs all are affected negatively in regulated markets.

Perhaps what is most vexing about rent control is that its interference in the market creates windfalls that fall in directions different from the intended distributional consequences. Those who end up in rent controlled units are not necessarily those who value them most or who are most in need of low-cost housing. Some tenants are advantaged by history—they have lived in rent controlled units for a long period of time. Others are willing to pay more than the legally allowed rent for the opportunity to live in an apartment. For these tenants, rent control may make little difference in the total cost of renting an apartment. When an apartment is sublet, windfall gains are likely to be earned by tenants holding the lease who can ask for bonus payments. In the case of new leases, landlords can take advantage of the reduced supply of controlled apartments by being more selective of tenants or demanding side payments.

For many, all of the problems and inefficiencies created by rent regulations could be excused if other social goals were met. Most prominent among these goals is the use of rent regulations to achieve a more equal and socially desirable distribution of income. But if this is the argument on which advocates of rent regulations must rely, it too must fail. Rent control is inequitable in the way it distributes costs and in the manner in which it distributes subsidies.

The benefits of rent regulations are not income conditioned. Rather, they are a function of the quality of the housing stock itself. The larger the margin between the regulated rent and the rent that could be charged in an unregulated market, the greater the size of the benefit realized by tenants living in regulated units. Thus, the size of this benefit is determined by the characteristics and location of the apartment and not the income of the occupants. It is entirely possible for these benefits to be highest for higher income households because these households move less frequently, giving landlords fewer opportunities to upgrade rents. On the other hand, the poor and elderly are more likely to be found living in rent controlled units, so in aggregate, they command more benefits.[41]

Only 14 percent of the occupied rental housing stock in New York City is not covered by rent regulations.[42] Thus, many non-poor renters will live in units that are controlled. The 1984 New York City Housing and Vacancy Survey identified more households with income over $20,000 per year living in rent stabilized apartments than households with incomes less than $20,000. Nearly 80 percent of the 56,000 households earning $35,000 or more annually are paying less than 20 percent of their income in rent, an indication that regulations do not target benefits very efficiently.

On the other hand, despite a significant share of the benefits of rent regulations leaking out to affluent households, many of the poor do live in rent regulated units. The 1983 median income of residents of rent controlled units was $11,000, 15 percent below the median income of all New York City renters. It is worth noting that the median income of renters in public housing projects, where occupancy is income conditioned, is $7,000, far below the median for any controlled status housing in the private market. In all, approximately 86 percent of poor and near poor residents live in either controlled or stabilized apartments. Thus, many poor households pay lower rents under rent regulations.

Two caveats to this distribution of benefits reduce their meaningfullness in terms of evaluating rent control as a successful income transfer program. First, even though many poor tenants are recipients of the benefits from living in rent regulated apartments, not all face housing costs that can be considered affordable. Nearly 220,000 poor households face rental burdens that exceed 35 percent of their income. Given the tightness of the rental market, a problem critics of rent control credit to the controls themselves, alternative housing opportunities do not exist. The second caveat concerns the condition of the regulated stock. If housing suppliers are undermaintaining structures because of restrictions on the rental income they can collect, lower controlled rents may be accompanied by lower housing quality.

There are few issues that can attract virtually unanimous critical opinion among housing economists—rent regulation is one that does. Although it is difficult to establish empirically each of the negative impacts of rent regulations upon housing markets, there is little doubt as to the direction of their contributing effect. The one virtue of rent controls is that they provide distributional relief to the poorest households in society. They do so, however, in an extremely inefficient way. Numerous high-income households manage to enjoy the benefits of regulated rents. Further, the size of the rent-regulated benefit is a function of housing choice; benefits are not income conditioned. Even if we were willing to withstand the amount of leakage, it is far from clear that those who lose from rent controls are the group from which we would prefer to transfer resources.

6

Housing Market Trends

Effective policy planning requires an understanding of the various forces and trends that are likely to shape the structure of the housing market into the next century. Although accurate predictions about the future course of housing market events are fraught with uncertainty, they can provide a baseline for planning purposes. This chapter focuses on trends in housing demand, changes in household composition, and the aging of the state's population.

Projected Housing Demand[43]

In this section we develop a number of estimates of future housing demand for the ten housing regions in New York State. These projections are compared to existing housing resources and historical records of building construction to identify potential regional supply shortages. Regions where housing demand outstrips supply may be particularly vulnerable to affordability problems.

The housing demand projections are based on the detailed population projections made in the *New York State Project 2000 Population Report*. The *Project 2000 Population Report* estimates that 18.5 million people will be living in New York State by the year 2000, nearly 1 million more people than the 1980 population.[44] To estimate future levels of housing demand, these population projections are combined with two estimates of average household size based on historical trends.

The baseline estimate of housing demand for the year 2000 is calculated by dividing the projected New York State population by the average household size of 1980. In 1980, average household size in New York State was 2.77 persons per household. Using the *Population Report* mid-range estimate of 5.6 percent population growth to the year 2000 yields an increase in the demand for housing of 356,000 units, to nearly 6.7 million units, if household size remains the same.

This number is likely to be an underestimate of the true number of households because average household size has been declining since the 1960s and is likely to decline further by the end of the century. The aging of the state's population, the increasing wealth of its residents, and a continuation of the set of complex sociological factors determining family formation are likely to result in a continued decline in household size.[45] For the high-range demand estimate we assume that the post-1950 regional rate of decline in household size continues. This assumes that households will be 17 percent smaller on average and that the number of households will increase to more than 8 million by the year 2000. This represents an increase of nearly 1.4 million households over the baseline estimate. The baseline and high-range estimates will likely bracket the actual number of households in the year 2000.

Housing analysts generally agree that well-functioning housing markets require that five percent of the units be vacant in order to accommodate the flux of mobile households.[46] Applying the five percent vacancy factor to our projected number of households yields a total estimated increase in housing demand for 374,000 units, using the baseline assumption. A total increase in demand for 1.47 million additional units results if continued declines in household size are assumed.

To accommodate this increased demand, New York State would have to enjoy net housing construction rates of between 19,000 and 76,000 units a year, witness the conversion of many larger units into smaller multiple dwellings, or experience lower population growth than predicted. 19,000 units is well within the statewide delivery capabilities of both private and public sources of construction, as evidenced by the rate of new additions to the stock over the last three decades. 76,000 additional units per year creates a more serious challenge. New York State has experienced this level of construction for short periods of time in the post-War era, but never has been able to sustain this rate during the past two decades. This suggests that a potential supply "shortage" could develop.

Even these high estimates may understate future housing needs. First, the estimates of the required annual increase are net of demolitions and conversions. Success at meeting these goals will depend, in part, on the extent to which the rate of housing demolition is reduced. New York State lost five percent of its existing housing stock from 1970 to 1980. This loss was particularly severe in New York City (eight percent) and other central cities (eight percent), and smallest in rural areas (one percent). The average annual loss totalled almost 25,000 units. If this rate continued, the number of units required by the year 2000 would increase by 500,000.

There is no way of knowing whether the rate of housing demolition and conversion will continue at this level through the end of the century, however, a number of factors suggest it will not. Census data indicate that population outmigration from central cities has stabilized in the first half of the 1980s, slowing the rate of reduction in demand experienced in the prior decade. Both residential and commercial developers have shown interest in inner city areas that for decades have been considered inappropriate for redevelopment. In addition, much of the poorest housing stock already has been demolished. The housing that remains is newer, higher quality, and less likely to be demolished in the near future. Based on these trends, we assume that residential conversions and demolitions will balance for the rest of this century, allowing us to focus solely on the level of new construction. If demolitions exceed conversions, our figures will be overly optimistic.

Estimates of the state's ability to keep pace with the increase in housing demand must be further qualified, because the present projections do not distinguish between units on the basis of housing quality. A 1984 DHCR study, "An Analysis of the Housing Needs for New York State," estimated that in 1980, 15 percent of the existing stock, or nearly 1 million units, were substandard.[47] Including replacements of substandard units in the projections would double the size of the housing gap. It is not clear whether substandard units should be included, however. Standard housing is clearly preferred to inadequate housing. Yet, when confronted with the choice, many people are content with choosing lower quality, lower cost housing, preferring it to better quality, higher priced alternatives.[48] Therefore, estimates are not adjusted for substandard housing; this implies that not all of the available supply will be standard housing (and additional maintenance may be required to maintain the quality of the existing housing stock).

On the other hand, it is entirely possible that the trends that lead to rapidly diminishing household sizes of the 1960s and 1970s will ease in the future. Preliminary data on 1980 patterns indicate a slowing in the rate of decline of household size. How these patterns will change over the next two decades is impossible to predict with certainty.

Further, housing "shortages" tend to be self regulating. If the number of available units falls short of the number of households, prices will rise. Increased housing prices will serve to dampen some of the demand and induce new supply. Over time, the "shortage" is likely to dissolve. In any event, the no-decline and rapid decline estimates used in this analysis are likely to bracket the true effects.[49]

We have identified two possible sources of increased number of households: more people and smaller household sizes. If household size does not change, the entire growth in the number of households will be due to population increases. If household size continues to decline at the rapid rate used for our high-end estimate, approximately 25 percent of the increase in numbers of households will be due to changes in the number of people in the state and 75 percent of the increase to diminution in household size. Accounting for changing household size increases the demand for housing units four-fold by the turn of the century. If household size declines more slowly, our estimated demand for housing is reduced proportionately.

Statewide estimates provide a convenient summary of the aggregation of many sub-housing markets, but they run the risk of masking regional differences. To examine this possibility, projections were made for each of the housing regions. Each estimate was based on the regional population projection, along with the region-specific pattern of household size change based on the pattern of decline experienced over the last two decades. These estimates were then applied to the projected regional population figures to derive the total number of households. Table 13 indicates the projected increase in housing demand to the Year 2000 for each region. It also indicates the percentage of such change attributable to projected population growth versus declining household size.

Regional results will vary from the average state experience because of different population growth and household formation rates. For example, the Buffalo region, which includes Erie County, is projected to lose population over the next two decades, while the Mid-Hudson region (Dutchess, Orange, and Ulster Counties) is projected to experience the fastest population growth in the state. Different regions will have different age and socioeconomic profiles, so they are unlikely to experience the same changes in average household size to the year 2000 (Figure 14).

Table 13 breaks the ten state regions into three groups. Group 1, consisting of Buffalo and the Southern Tier, is predicted to experience increased housing demand from 1980 to 2000 appreciably below the statewide average of approximately 22 percent.[50] Weaker housing demand in these two regions can be attributed to different factors. The Buffalo region is expected to experience a population decline of approximately three percent, but shrinking household size will be sufficient to generate a net increase in housing demand of 14 percent. The Southern Tier's projected household increase of 10.4 percent is a result of higher population growth rates combined with a continuation of an historically relatively stable average household size. Thus, population increases will have a stronger impact on household formation rates in the Southern Tier than they will for the state as a whole.

At the other extreme, both the North Country region and the Mid-

TABLE 13

PROJECTED INCREASE IN HOUSING DEMAND TO YEAR 2000*

REGION	% CHANGE 1980-2000	PERCENT CHANGE ATTRIBUTE TO:	
		POPULATION COMPONENT	HOUSEHOLD SIZE COMPONENT
LOW GROWTH			
BUFFALO	14%	-3%	103%
SOUTHERN TIER	10	37	63
AVERAGE GROWTH			
ROCHESTER	23	37	63
SYRACUSE	21	29	71
UPPER HUDSON	24	29	71
NEW YORK CITY	24	11	89
NORTH NYC SUBURBS	22	30	70
LONG ISLAND	19	52	48
HIGH GROWTH			
NORTH COUNTRY	33	55	45
MID-HUDSON	35	57	43
NEW YORK STATE	22%	24%	76%

*Based on declining household size assumption.

Hudson region (Ulster, Sullivan, Dutchess, and Orange counties) are forecast to experience growth in housing demand approximately 35-45 percent higher than the statewide average. These two regions are expected to have the state's most rapidly growing population. Changes in household size are projected to decline slower than the overall state average.

The middle grouping in the table consists of those regions whose future housing demand is within 20 percent of the state average. With the exception of Long Island, the primary source of change is the predicted decrease in average household size. Recall, however, that household

FIGURE 14

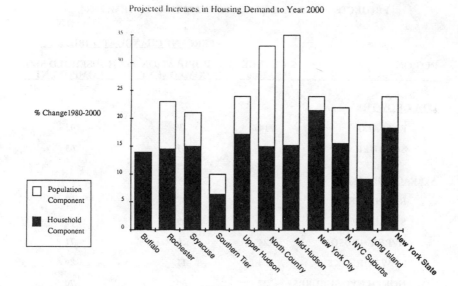

Projected Increases in Housing Demand to Year 2000

growth at the state average is likely to leave regional supply far short of demand.

Under the lower household growth assumption (i.e., that household size does not continue to decline) the groupings look little different. Changes in demand, under this assumption, can be derived from Table 13 by multiplying the percentage change in column 2 by the population component in column 3. New York City is the one housing region whose status would change markedly because of its predicted relatively stable population growth. If the average size of households does not continue to decline, New York City's projected housing demand increase is less than three percent.

Given the projected regional rates of housing demand, how tight will housing markets be by the year 2000? As a first cut, estimates of future housing demand are compared with historical data on trends in housing construction. This exercise is necessarily crude. Most importantly, the analysis cannot account for the complex, simultaneous interactions between supply and demand. The trend analysis is unable to account for changes in relative prices or wealth effects. To illustrate, if the relative price of housing should increase over the next two decades, perhaps because of supply shortages, it is likely that fewer new households will form.

Conversely, unanticipated increases in household wealth would lead to even greater levels of new household formation. For instance, increased statewide job creation would be one source of increased household demand for housing.

Despite its crudeness, the analysis is nevertheless instructive. Table 14 contains data on year-round housing construction by region over the last two decades. The last column contains the annual average number of units necessary to meet the projected number of households, plus the five percent vacancy increment. These estimates assume that the number of residential conversions will balance demolitions.

Comparisons between the average annual increase in projected housing demand and historical increases in supply reveal that New York City, the North Country, and Mid-Hudson regions are likely to experience increases in housing demand that exceed historical annual supply. To the extent that demolitions are correlated with the age of the stock, New York

TABLE 14

AVERAGE ANNUAL YEAR ROUND HOUSING UNIT PRODUCTION
BY CONSTRUCTION DATE,
NEW YORK STATE REGIONS: 1980

	1979 - March 1980	1975 - 1978	1970 - 1974	1960 - 1969	Annual Average Need to Year 2000
BUFFALO	4,403	4,435	6,654	6,053	3,190
ROCHESTER	3,536	5,167	8,331	6,761	3,966
SYRACUSE	4,553	5,378	7,373	6,164	3,971
SOUTHERN TIER	5,166	5,931	8,070	5,679	1,970
UPPER HUDSON	4,397	4,674	7,395	4,737	3,793
NORTH COUNTRY	2,945	2,849	3,900	2,316	3,030
MID HUDSON	3,605	4,224	5,717	4,232	4,266
NEW YORK CITY	17,345	16,256	25,336	40,397	32,904
NORTH NYC SUBURBS	3,400	4,051	6,987	8,229	4,546
LONG ISLAND	6,487	8,819	14,740	18,470	7,680

SOURCE: 1984-85 New York State Statistical Yearbook, p. 53, Table B-5.

City and the North Country might be pinched even further than what is suggested here, because of the greater prevalence in these two regions of older, less adequate housing.

Projections for Long Island and the Northern Suburbs indicate the possibility that housing demand will exceed supply, if new construction continues at its current pace. Other regions have shown the historical capacity to meet projected household increases.

Household Composition Trends

The projections above provide some quantitative evidence of a potential demand-supply imbalance that could further exacerbate affordability problems in New York State. The extent to which this actually happens will also depend on two important trends in the composition of state households: increasing numbers of female-headed households and the growth in aged households. From 1960-1980, New York State experienced a sharp rise in the number of families maintained by women with no spouse present. In fact, the strength of this phenomenon was so great that from 1960-1980, almost the entire growth in the number of New York State households was due to non-traditional household types.[51] Demographers forecast continued relative growth in the non-traditional household category.

Female-headed households are five times more likely than all other families to be poor.[52] Affordability is a particular problem of those in poverty—over 80 percent of the poor spend more than 40 percent of their income on housing services. Nearly 50 percent of households within 150 percent of the poverty line spend this much. Thus, the demography of poverty has increasingly involved single heads of households. This trend in household formation portends future affordability problems.

A second important demographic trend is the aging of the state's population. Over half of the population growth in New York from 1980-2000 will be accounted for by an increase in the aged population. This will be true especially in the suburbs as the population ages in place. Policy makers must be sensitive to the implications of a changing age structure when designing housing policy.

Many of the elderly are susceptible to changes in housing costs because of their reliance on retirement income. Some of the elderly are protected from housing cost changes through rent regulations and state governmental programs designed to relieve housing cost burdens. However, these programs do not cover all elderly homeowners, nor do they cover all cost increases. Unfortunately, property value appreciation has provided little relief; elderly homeowners are, for the most part, unable to liquify their home equity because of restrictions in the state's banking laws and are unable to defer their property tax bills until their estate is settled or their house is sold, as they can in some other states.

Increasing numbers of the old-old (those over 75) will present a third policy challenge for the next century. People in this age group are more likely to have low incomes, require health care and other services, and be living without help. A range of innovative housing alternatives (including but not limited to congregate care) that are not shared to any significant extent by other population subgroups have been proposed to allow the old-old to continue living outside of institutions. New York State has begun to investigate ways of increasing the range of housing options available to the aged. Further efforts, and broader participation by nongovernmental actors, will be needed to keep abreast of these demographic shifts.

7

Housing Policy Options

State and local governments in New York run a myriad of programs aimed at improving the state's housing stock and increasing housing choices. New and innovative programs are continually being developed and added to the existing set of regulatory and expenditure programs. The resulting housing policy is a multifaceted approach, targeting resources to various areas of the state and to different types of households.

Currently, too little is known about the relative cost effectiveness of these various programs. Our measures of success—how many households are helped, how many structures are completed, how many units are rehabilitated, how many mortgages are written, etc.—are far too crude to enable policy makers to determine how best to spend the next tax dollar on housing policy. Nevertheless, the demands for public intervention in the housing market are so great that policy makers have proceeded without full knowledge of program effects. Far more work is required to analyze the full costs and benefits of the various policy options, but comprehensive policy evaluation and analysis is a luxury frequently dispensed with in the policy making process.

The following sections examine a variety of policy options for ameliorating New York State's housing affordability quandary. These policies might reduce high housing cost burdens through either increasing the purchasing capabilities of some families or by reducing the cost of housing services. A number of policy options that would reduce the level of rent regulations are also examined.

Demand Side Policies[53]

In many respects, the housing affordability problem is one of too little household income. As households move through the income ladder, the incidence of excessive housing cost burdens diminishes. Of course, there will always be some households whose desire for quality housing is so strong that they will be willing to incur excessive housing cost burdens even with high incomes. But these households are not generally considered targets for public concern, and we can ignore them when formulating policy.

By defining the affordability problem as a shortage of resources, our analysis focuses on ways of increasing household income. We should recognize, however, that policies that increase household income will not necessarily lead to increased housing consumption. Nor will they necessarily lead households to improve housing quality.[54] The observed income elasticity of demand for housing, that is, the percentage change in housing consumption resulting from a one percent change in income, indicates that households will spend a portion of any increases in income on other commodities.[55]

The state can attempt to construct policies that tie resource awards to changes in housing consumption. But, unless strict control is exerted on the use of these funds, we can expect leakages into other sectors. Experience has proven strict control to be administratively difficult, if not impossible. Nevertheless, even if subsidized households fail to change their housing consumption choices, the effect of increasing housing resources will be to reduce housing cost burdens.

As in other areas of public policy, the state can increase household resources and facilitate the access of poor households to affordable housing by pursuing policies that lead to economic growth and development. Surely this should be and is a major policy concern. Beyond this general prescription for economic prosperity, however, what can the state do to assist low- and moderate-income households' demand for housing?

Housing Allowance for AFDC recipients

New York State currently provides households receiving Aid for Dependent Children (AFDC) additional funds for housing, based on household size and prevailing housing costs. This housing allowance, recently increased for only the second time since 1974, still falls short of covering housing costs in most neighborhoods. For instance, in New York City the AFDC housing allowance is currently set at approximately two-thirds of the Section 8 determined fair market rent. Presumably, the tenant is expected to use the non-shelter portion of the AFDC allowance to cover the remaining one-third of the rent bill. A major virtue of this program from the state perspective is its financing arrangement. Providing housing allowances tied to AFDC payments shifts one-half of program costs backward to the federal government and one-quarter forward to county governments. Thus, the state provides four dollars of coverage for each dollar it spends.

Housing allowances add to the income of recipient households and can be used to purchase better quality housing. These subsidies, however, are not sufficient to cover the entire rent burden. Nor will increases in the allowance necessarily lead to greater housing consumption. AFDC housing allowances are best thought of as a type of general income support program, rather than a specific housing program.

One option that would increase recipient expenditures on housing would be to transfer AFDC housing allowance payments directly to landlords. This would circumvent some leakage into other purchases. But efforts to pay landlords directly have been restricted by federal law, and interfere with recipient choices. Thus, policy makers are faced with a tradeoff between higher housing consumption and lower household housing expense ratios. Even if this tradeoff is made successfully, the AFDC housing allowance add-on only addresses a small segment of the affordability problem in that it fails to reach non-AFDC households.

Rental Subsidies

One mechanism for closing the housing gap is to develop a state financed rental subsidy. Rental subsidies can be structured to provide differential household support depending on household size, income, and housing market characteristics. As is the case of other demand side programs, the impact of rental subsidies will depend on a number of factors. The evidence from the Experimental Housing Allowance Program indicates that whether rental subsidies are used to upgrade housing choices, purchase other commodities, or result in higher rents that are captured by landlords (or some combination of these) is generally determined by the characteristics of the housing market and the behavior of participating households. Undoubtedly, tighter administrative control can also influence the allocation of effects.[56]

The cost of the rental subsidy program examined here is based on the housing cost gap estimates presented in chapter 4. This subsidy would provide low-income renters access to moderate quality apartments at a cost no greater than 30 percent of household income.[57] The 30 percent cost standard is based on the generally accepted standard for federal programs, although this standard, as well as any other, is arbitrary. The gap between household income and affordable rents was estimated in chapter 4 to exceed $1.8 billion annually (1980 dollars).[58] Undoubtedly, this gap would grow larger as households reconfigure their housing choices in line with the incentives that a housing subsidy program creates.

To conduct a subsidy program of this magnitude would require an extremely large budget allocation, almost an order of magnitude larger than current state housing expenditures. However, a variety of adjustments could be made to run a more limited program and reduce the size of these outlays.[59] For instance, a rental subsidy program could be restricted to only those families whose household income left them below the poverty line. Targeting subsidies in this way reduces the potential number of participants by 36 percent and reduces aggregate annual costs by nearly 30 percent to $1.3 billion. If households are required to contribute 40 percent of their income in rent, rather than the 30 percent standard, the size of the rental subsidy program is reduced from $1.8 billion to $1.5 billion. A program that only provided access to a unit renting at the 25th percentile would cost $1.1 billion.

Absent a change in federal policies that would provide significant additional assistance, it is unlikely that the state would fund annual housing allowances of this magnitude. It is more likely that the state would fund a more moderately sized subsidy program. As an example, we examine the extent of program penetration for budget outlays of $50 million or $100 million (1980 dollars). This would correspond to a budget of approximately $70 to $140 million in 1988 dollars and would require a sizable increase in current housing expenditures.

Limiting program size requires that we develop some mechanism for choosing subsidy recipients. One option targets the subsidy to those households who are least able to afford adequate housing. Table 15 examines the extent of program coverage for subsidy plans aimed at the most needy households. Only 1.3 percent of potential recipients would be covered under a $50 million allocation and 2.8 percent would be covered under the $100 million allocation, if all renters under 150 percent of the poverty line are eligible.[60]

An alternative approach is to provide rental subsidies to those most able to help themselves, and reserve other forms of housing assistance, such as public housing, for those most in need. This program would first provide assistance to those with the smallest cost gaps.[61] By helping those households with incomes at the higher end of the qualifying pool, a $50 million program would then cover 10.5 percent of potential recipients. For $100 million, 15.7 percent of potential recipients could be funded (see Table 16). Table 15 and 16 also contain estimates of program coverage for a subsidy program that bases rental subsidies on the cost of renting a housing unit at the 25th percentile. Smaller average subsidies let the dollars stretch farther but still leave program coverage far short of universal.

When compared with current New York State budget outlays, these numbers indicate how far we are from being able to provide a universal subsidy program. The potential need for rental subsidies outstrips the

TABLE 15

**HOUSING SUBSIDY PROGRAM TARGETED AT MOST NEEDY RECIPIENTS:
PERCENT ELIGIBLE COVERED**

| | PROGRAM SIZE (1980 Dollars) | | | |
| | $50 MILLION | | $100 MILLION | |
	100% Poverty	150% Poverty	100% Poverty	150% Poverty
RENTERS (30% Standard)* (median unit)	2.0%	1.3%	4.5%	1.4%
RENTERS (40% Standard)** (median unit)	2.2	1.5	5.0	2.8
RENTERS (30% Standard)* (25th pct unit)	2.8%	2.0%	6.4%	4.3%
RENTERS (40% Standard)** (25th pct unit)	3.3	2.4	7.2	5.2

*Renters contribute 30% of income to housing costs.
**Renters contribute 40% of income to housing costs.

state's ability to fund them and will continue to do so annually. Nevertheless, rental subsidies would enable some lower income households to gain access to higher quality housing or to relieve excessively high housing-cost burdens.

Mortgage Subsidies

For many years it has been national housing policy to encourage home ownership; this goal has also been pursued by state policy makers. Home ownership is believed to engender a number of socially desirable behaviors that have positive external effects on others. In particular, there is evidence of the level of property maintenance and care in a community being positively related to the level of ownership.[62]

This section examines the potential of a mortgage subsidy program to provide housing cost relief. The conceivable number of recipients for a home ownership subsidy is large unless some restrictions are placed on

TABLE 16

HOUSING SUBSIDY PROGRAM TARGETED AT
MAXIMUM NUMBER OF RECIPIENTS:
PERCENT ELIGIBLE COVERED

	PROGRAM SIZE (1980 Dollars)			
	$50 MILLION		$100 MILLION	
	100% Poverty	150% Poverty	100% Poverty	150% Poverty
RENTERS (30% Standard)* (median unit)	10.6%	10.5%	16.5%	15.7%
RENTERS (40% Standard)** (median unit)	13.8	13.9	21.1	20.7
RENTERS (30% Standard)* (25th pct unit)	16.3%	14.7%	25.3%	24.3%
RENTERS (40% Standard)** (25th pct unit)	22.0	24.0	33.3	34.9

*Renters contribute 30% of income to housing costs.
**Renters contribute 40% of income to housing costs.

who is eligible for support. It is assumed that households below the poverty line would be excluded from this program because their income prospects make them unlikely to be able to carry the financial responsibilities of owning a home. Evidence from previous efforts at providing ownership subsidies for poor households indicates high default rates for this group. At the other end of the income scale, we exclude from consideration those households whose income exceeds 150 percent of the poverty line. This restricts recipients to be below the median income—a level that is sufficient to purchase the median-priced unit without subsidy.[63]

Eligible households can be assisted in their attempt to own a home through a mortgage subsidy program similar in concept to the rental subsidy program discussed above. SONYMA does this by taking advantage of its tax exempt borrowing status to float debt at rates below that of taxable issues and uses the proceeds to write lower than market rate mortgages for qualifying households. Consider that on a SONYMA $60,000, 30-year mortgage, the monthly payments at seven percent are

$400, which is $125 less than the payments for a comparable, market rate ten percent mortgage.

Mortgage subsidies have been favored by first-time, moderate-income home buyers in the state but are being phased out by the Tax Reform Act of 1986.[64] The state can choose to continue to provide home ownership relief by directly subsidizing market rate mortgages after the tax favored status expires, but only by incurring direct budget costs.

To develop a sense of the possible budget costs of directly subsidizing home ownership through mortgage subsidies, suppose the state allocated $50 million (1980 dollars) to assist low-income renters to purchase homes. If these homes were valued at the median price in the region, and owners were required to devote 40 percent of household income to their mortgage payments, $50 million in mortgage subsidies would be sufficient to subsidize 28 percent of the 233,000 renter households with income between 100 percent and 150 percent of the poverty line. Whether the state provided this subsidy through a private lender or holds the mortgage itself is equally costly to the state budget. The opportunity cost of holding below market rate loans is just as expensive as the direct subsidy, although only the latter will appear as an expenditure in the budget.

Of course, partial coverage of the potential recipient population is no reason to forgo running this program. Many federal programs are funded far below full coverage levels. However, the lack of coverage provided by a program of even this size gives some sense of the magnitude of the task ahead.

Up-Front Capital Grants

An alternative approach to mortgage subsidies is to provide up-front capital grants to specified households.[65] These grants would reduce the borrowing requirements for potential homeowners. Many moderate income households can afford the carrying costs of a mortgage, but are excluded from the ownership market by their inability to accumulate sufficient savings to cover closing and downpayment costs.

To estimate the potential cost of a capital subsidy program, attention is again restricted to households with income between 100 percent and 150 percent of the poverty line. The maximum mortgage payments these households could make is calculated using the 40 percent income standard, taking into account average property tax and insurance requirements. This payment determines the household's borrowing capacity. The difference between the size of the mortgage the household can afford and the median-priced structure in their housing region equals the size of the capital subsidy in this analysis.

Table 17 contains the results of this exercise, using the median value unit as the standard for determining the size of the grant, and assuming mortgage rates of ten percent. As can be seen, the mortgage borrowing capacity of households in this income range is limited. At a minimum, the up-front capital grants must make up 47 percent of the purchase price of the median valued home in the North Country. In most other regions, the capital grant would need to make up approximately 60 percent of the purchase price. The importance of incorporating the effect of insurance and tax payments is clearly seen in the northern New York City suburbs. On average, targeted households in this region have a relatively low mortgage capacity because high median housing prices dictate that limited household income be allocated to insurance and taxes.

TABLE 17

UP-FRONT CAPITAL GRANTS FOR MEDIAN VALUE UNIT
(1980 DOLLARS)

REGION	MEDIAN VALUE*	AVERAGE MORTGAGE CAPACITY**	CAPITAL GRANT	PROGRAM COST***
BUFFALO	$37,500	$14,000	$23,500	$566,350,000
ROCHESTER	42,500	14,700	27,800	417,000,000
SYRACUSE	37,500	15,000	22,500	508,500,000
SOUTHERN TIER	32,500	16,500	16,000	332,800,000
UPPER HUDSON	37,500	14,000	23,500	397,150,000
NORTH COUNTRY	32,500	17,500	15,000	175,500,000
MID HUDSON	42,500	15,500	27,000	342,800,000
NEW YORK CITY	52,500	12,000	40,500	11,749,050,000
NORTH NYC SUBURBS	77,500	6,000	71,500	1,222,650,000
LONG ISLAND	52,500	16,000	36,500	689,850,000
				$16,401,750,000

*Midpoint of $5,000 grouping
**Based on 30 year loan at 10%
***Assumes full participation
Calculated from 1980 PUMS data

The result is that program costs for providing state-wide capital grants is extremely high. Even a program funded at the $100 million level would be able to assist less than one percent of the qualifying households between 100 percent and 150 percent of the poverty line.

The potential impact of this program would be greatly increased if interest rates were lower. Lower borrowing rates increase the mortgage capacity of homeowners, thereby reducing the requirements for the capital grant. For instance, if eight percent mortgage money was available to purchasers, the mortgage capacity of borrowers would increase 36 percent from $14,000 to $19,000. This reduces the up-front grant requirements by over 20 percent, allowing greater program penetration. Wealthier households would require smaller grants and result in higher coverage rates or lower program cost. But wealthier households also are better able to save and finance their homes without assistance.

Undoubtedly, a capital grant program of this type would be likely to change a number of incentives that would affect housing markets. For example, capital grants are likely to reduce the household incentives to save for downpayments. It is difficult to recommend this approach for encouraging home ownership without knowing more about the effect of these grants on household decisions to save, the size of the potential pool that could be serviced, or housing prices.

Up-front capital grants are one-time expenditures that can involve sizable budgetary totals. In theory, it should be no more costly to write down mortgage costs through the use of a capital grant than to subsidize mortgage payments, as long as the state faces the same cost of borrowing as individuals. However, up-front grants may involve lower administrative costs because they only require a one-time determination rather than an annual administrative process.

On the other hand, the value of up-front grants can be captured entirely by the recipient of the grant, unlike annual subsidy awards. If a grant recipient chooses to sell his home shortly after purchase, he would be able to cash out the public's investment in home ownership. What was intended as a public resource becomes a private gain. Program design should incorporate some provision to recapture this sizable subsidy in the case where recipients seek to sell their homes. Although this feature would increase administrative costs, it would provide a mechanism for keeping these funds targeted.

Utility Cost Subsidies

New York State also can provide demand size assistance by helping households with other components of their housing expenses. One way is to help low-income households meet their utility bills by expanding the eligibility and payment terms of existing programs.[66]

The potential for relieving housing cost burdens by subsidizing utility costs is large and varies considerably across the state (Table 18). Utility costs differ as a percentage of household income depending on the type and source of power, the climate, the demand of households, and the quality of the building stock. Different subsidy approaches will have different incentive effects on recipients across the state.

TABLE 18

ANNUAL UTILITY COSTS BY REGION AND TENURE (1980):
DOLLAR COSTS AND PERCENT FOR WHOM UTILITY COSTS
EXCEED 40% OF INCOME

REGION	MEAN OWNER COSTS		MEAN RENTER COSTS	
	dollar cost	% for whom utility costs exceed 40% of income	dollar cost	% for whom utility costs exceed 40% of income
BUFFALO	$1,247	2.2%	$667	6.3%
ROCHESTER	1,331	2.0	498	4.8
SYRACUSE	1,332	2.7	592	4.8
SOUTHERN TIER	1,228	3.1	580	5.3
UPPER HUDSON	1,399	2.4	640	6.0
NORTH COUNTRY	1,362	4.2	665	7.4
MID HUDSON	1,611	5.0	696	5.9
NEW YORK CITY	1,870	4.7	366	5.2
NORTH NYC SUBURBS	1,993	2.3	485	2.9
LONG ISLAND	1,902	2.8	705	5.3

Calculated from 1980 PUMS data.

Although a general income subsidy based on utility usage would reduce the housing cost burden for all tenants, it makes sense to reduce heating cost burdens by making energy savings improvements, because of the recurring nature of utility costs. Unfortunately, tenants have little incentive to invest in insulation. Owners of most rental structures also have little incentive to invest in energy saving devices because tenants pay utility bills. Investment most likely will occur if market conditions allow recapture of the investment through higher than normal rents.[67]

Although subsidizing utility bills directly can reduce the housing cost burden for many households, it also may lead subsidized households to increase their energy consumption or switch to different energy sources. Consider heating costs in the North Country, by far the least temperate of the housing regions. Despite bone chilling cold, average utility costs are far below warmer downstate regions. In part, this reflects lower utility costs. But it also reflects the widespread use of alternative heating sources. If a subsidy program was to change the relative price of a specific energy source, upstate households might switch their heating choices.

An alternative approach is to tie assistance to the installation of energy-saving improvements. This approach was tried through the use of tax credits in the federal income tax code, but most of the benefits were enjoyed by middle- and upper-income households. Utility cost subsidies undoubtedly will have a greater impact on the efficiency of energy usage than on changing the affordability of housing. Any evaluation of this policy must incorporate these multiple goals.

Property Tax Subsidies

Property taxes can also add to housing cost burdens, particularly for those households with high property wealth and presently low levels of income. New York State currently uses circuit breakers and local homestead relief provisions to reduce the property tax burdens of certain households. Circuit breakers operate through the state income tax by refunding a portion of the locally imposed excess property taxes when the property tax to household income ratio exceeds a legislated threshold. Localities use the homestead exemption to reduce the assessed portion of single family homes subject to local property taxes. These programs could be expanded to provide further relief.

New York State can change the circuit breaker program directly and make it more generous (presumably at the budgetary expense of a number of other state programs). The circuit breaker could be extended to many more households who would qualify for subsidy, but who fail to apply because of ignorance of the program or because they do not file state tax returns otherwise. Some increased program coverage could be financed by better targeting of program benefits on income conditioned grounds. Currently, circuit breaker relief reduces state tax collections by over $20 million.

The impact of these changes on state resources will depend on how households change their housing consumption patterns, because the size of the circuit breaker depends, in part, on housing values. The circuit breaker has the effect of reducing property taxes, thereby reducing the cost of housing for both renters and owners.[68] For qualifying households, the reduction in the marginal property tax liability can be as great as 50 percent. Since the price elasticity of demand for housing is positive, this will result in encouraging state tax payers to consume somewhat more housing, thus driving up program costs.

The circuit breaker also has the effect of making local property tax increases less costly for those who receive the subsidy. This may also increase existing program costs if local governments attempt to pass their financing costs on to the state. One consequence of this shifting in the source of finance of local services is that the circuit breaker results in a distribution of state resources to high property tax, high house value regions (holding income constant).[69]

Summary

The underlying premise for demand side subsidies is that the housing problem is primarily one of resources—decent housing is simply too expensive for many New Yorkers. While many non-poor New Yorkers take on higher housing costs to be able to live in a more pleasant environment or to guarantee access to higher quality public services, far too many residents face crippling rent-to-income ratios because their incomes are so low.

Despite their high costs, demand side subsidies do not guarantee success. The evidence from the housing allowance experiments indicate that the use of rental vouchers can actually lead to higher housing prices in tight housing markets.[70] Thus, housing subsidy benefits would not be totally captured by the recipients. Further, it is possible that the availability of the subsidy will encourage families that formerly doubled up to live apart. While this would reduce rates of crowding, it also would have the impact of increasing the demand for low-income housing.

Supply Side Policies

An alternative approach for redressing the affordability problem is to encourage policies that would reduce the cost of providing housing. Reducing the costs of housing would enable more households to operate within the private non-subsidized market and allow subsidy dollars to reach more households.

The next section discusses two broad types of policy approaches for reducing the cost of housing. The first approach subsidizes housing producers to provide housing services at lower costs. Subsidizing suppliers is likely to have similar effects on the price and availability of housing as the demand side strategies examined above. However, in this case, the subsidy is provided to the developers—not the households. The second generic approach is in the area of regulatory reform. By reducing the regulatory requirements imposed on producers, the state can reduce the cost of developing housing.

An analysis of effective supply side strategies must begin with an understanding of how the cost of producing housing can be reduced. Housing construction costs fall into a number of different categories. Builders incur costs in site acquisition and planning, labor, building and material, financing, and meeting regulatory requirements on building quality and density. The importance of these costs varies across the state, depending on local market conditions. In general, financing costs vary less across the state than other cost components.[71] At the other extreme are the varying costs of land, depending on the location of the building site. The sum of these costs often exceeds the rent paying ability of lower income households. The gap between affordable rents and market rates can be bridged using a number of different approaches.

Subsidy Strategies

Financing Subsidies. Financing is a major cost component of building housing. The state has two options for subsidizing the borrowing costs of developers: either directly subsidize market rate finance or provide developers access to below market rate funds.

Currently the state subsidizes some developers of both single-family and multi-family housing. Single-family home finance subsidies are provided through SONYMA, which has devoted one-third of its funds for financing new construction. Although new construction adds to the stock of housing in the state, providing these funds directly to developers probably results in housing prices higher than they otherwise would be, because part of the value of tax-exempt financed borrowing is capitalized into the purchase price of the home when the financing is provided through the seller.[72] As a result, the value of the subsidy is captured by the supplier and not the household in need of affordable housing. By allowing the subsidy to be portable with the purchaser, as it is for the remaining two-thirds of the SONYMA funds, SONYMA could solve this problem and target the subsidy to the intended recipients.

Multi-family housing developers have access to below market rate mortgages through the bonding authority of the Housing Finance Agency. Funding is available to both not-for-profit and for-profit developers.

Although tax-exempt borrowing through HFA will not be phased out by the Tax Reform Act of 1986, the Tax Act imposes strict requirements on both the tenant mix and tenant incomes in for-profit developments. These requirements impose costs and create uncertainty for developers and reduce the attractiveness of this option. Until the full impacts of these requirements are understood we are unlikely to see much for-profit development using this tool.

Not-for-profit developers are not bound by the same tenant mix requirements. However, this sector is generally less skilled at putting together complex development projects and requires greater technical assistance. Although technical assistance can be costly to provide, the lower cost financing made possible by tax-exempt borrowing makes this a desirable option for state policy.

Land and Property Policy.   New York State and local governments own appreciable amounts of land. Although most of this land is not suitable for development, some of it might be used for housing, including land with abandoned but salvageable structures. Providing this land for affordable housing development, as is being done on a limited scale in many localities throughout the state, would reduce development costs and permit housing to be offered at lower prices. The state could also facilitate the land assemblage process by extending the powers of eminent domain. Developers cite the inability of obtaining large enough parcels of land as a hindrance to housing creation.

One major problem developers face is trying to acquire public land to develop affordable housing. Too often they find it difficult to identify the location of available parcels. State officials can ease the development process by rapidly developing inventories of the holdings of land that would be suitable for housing development.

Currently, not all publicly owned land can be used for housing, even if decision makers decide to use it for that purpose. County governments own sizable parcels of land but are unable to develop this land for housing because the State Constitution limits development powers to cities, towns, and villages. Amending the State Constitution to permit governments to develop housing would increase the amount of land available for affordable housing production.

Although some publicly held property has been used for the development of affordable housing, housing advocates are unhappy with the rate of speed with which properties are made available. Even though land and building grants to affordable housing developers appear quite attractive, the relinquishing of vacant land has a cost. The state forgoes revenues from the potential sale of vacant parcels or the potential benefits from developing them for other purposes. One mechanism that the state might use to maintain some policy flexibility would be to provide public land to housing developers through a long-term lease. By doing so, the state retains a future option to use the property in some other way.

Jurisdictions holding vacant land and facing an affordable housing shortage hold a potential policy instrument in their hands. However, whether land disposition strategies are more cost efficient than other incentive mechanisms for housing is not clear.

Tax Policy. Recent changes in federal tax law have made residential housing a less attractive investment for most investors. The combined effects of lower marginal tax rates, less generous depreciation rules, higher capital gains taxes, and the inability to offset income with passive losses all make rental real estate less attractive to own. The state can counter the effects of these changes in federal law by retaining more generous depreciation allowances or instituting some form of tax credit.

Such tax incentives will have limited use to non-profit developers, but they would increase the attractiveness of residential investment for for-profit development. Unless the state somehow ties these incentives to the mix of housing under development, there is no assurance that more affordable housing will flow directly to low- and moderate-income households. On the other hand, if program requirements were drawn too tightly, participation would become less attractive. Although probably not sufficiently large an inducement to stand by itself, tax policy could complement other types of inducements.

Capital Grants. New York State could provide further assistance to developers by expanding and extending existing programs that provide capital grants for housing construction. These programs reduce the up-front cash requirements and borrowing needs of housing suppliers, thereby allowing apartments to be offered at lower rents.

New York State has used the Low Income Housing Trust Fund to provide capital grants or no-interest loans to developers substantially rehabilitating or converting vacant structures for housing low-income households. Grants of up to $40,000 per unit can significantly decrease developers' costs and permit the development of low-cost housing. Similarly, the Housing Development Fund has been used to defray the start-up costs facing housing developers.

In theory, up-front capital grants need not have any different impact than mortgage subsidies on the ability of developers to provide affordable housing for low- and moderate-income renters. For those non-profit

developers experiencing difficulty raising sufficient capital to get projects
started, however, capital grants can be extremely useful. Unlike mortgage
subsidies, capital grants are made all at once and require larger, up-front,
budget allocations.

Energy Investment Credits. The state also could encourage the
development of lower cost housing by providing incentives to upgrade the
energy efficiency of new construction or extensive rehabilitation. Energy
efficiency upgrades would then lower the cost of operating these structures
in the future. Unlike annual energy assistance payments, this type of
program would enable the state to continually recoup a return on its
investment. Currently, such assistance is provided to the state's public
housing stock through the Home Energy Assistance Program, funded by
the federal government. A state funded program could be targeted to
developers of affordable housing. The cost effectiveness of this program
varies with the market price of energy. The relatively lower real energy
prices of the 1980s make this program less attractive today than a decade
ago, although this may change.

Insurance Costs. As with the other components of the operating
budget, expenditures on insurance ultimately get passed along to tenants
as higher rents. In the past, both the federal and state government have
been able to reduce insurance costs by filling in parts of the market where
the private sector has refused to enter. As an example, the SONYMA
mortgage insurance program, financed through a mortgage recording tax
surcharge, provides the assurance that private lenders need to make loans
to deteriorating neighborhoods. New York State could develop similar
insurance plans that could be extended to more households, thereby
attracting greater private lending activity. Similarly, direct assistance for
meeting insurance costs could be provided by the state, much in the same
way that rental payments are subsidized.

Infrastructure Investment. Especially in the state's less urbanized
areas, the cost of constructing new housing extends beyond the factors we
have identified above. In particular, new development cannot proceed
without infrastructure development (i.e., roads, sewers, water delivery
systems, etc.). In recent years, local governments have passed the entire
cost of infrastructure development onto developers. This greatly raises the
costs of developing new housing.

Given the limited public fisc in rural areas, the costs of infrastructure
development create a major obstacle to constructing affordable housing.
State activity in these regions could be directed usefully towards sharing
development costs. There is no cause, however, for the state to share in the

infrastructure costs of market rate housing. Local governments should be able to recoup at least some of the development costs from those units not intended to be subsidized.

Regulatory Strategies

Housing services are regulated in a number of different ways by New York State and its local units of government. These regulations fall into six major groupings:

a. regulations concerning land use;
b. regulations concerning building construction;
c. regulations concerning building maintenance;
d. regulations concerning environmental quality;
e. regulations concerning historic preservation;
f. regulations concerning contract rents.

Each of these regulatory codes has been developed with the goal of protecting some aspect of the public's welfare: land-use regulations separate incompatible uses, building codes seek to guarantee levels of health and safety, environmental regulations protect the state's natural resources, historic preservation seeks to preserve the state's architectural and cultural history, and rent controls shelter poor renters from high rents. Each of the codes has impacts beyond their intended targets, however, including consequences for the cost of providing housing services.

Much of the regulatory authority discussed in this section rests with local governments in New York State. Ironically, local autonomy was originally granted by the state, but it now precludes the state from acting unilaterally to alter these regulations. However, the state can develop incentives to encourage local governments to pursue broader statewide interests. For instance, the state could tie availability of state financing subsidies to regulatory reform by local governments. By encouraging localities to relax some of these regulatory requirements, the state can make the conditions for the construction of affordable housing more amenable. Similarly, the state could alter enabling legislation that would encourage localities to negotiate with developers over land-use outcomes rather than establish inflexible use requirements.[73]

Land-Use Regulations

Zoning powers in New York State are vested with local governments. Although originally established as a mechanism for separating conflicting or incompatible uses (e.g., residential development and heavy industry), zoning laws have increasingly been used as mechanisms for enforcing and stabilizing community standards.[74] Suburban communities have made use of zoning powers to maintain the "character of their neighborhoods," by restricting land use to low densities through a variety of zoning requirements, including minimum lot size and prohibition of multi-family dwellings. In many suburban communities zoning requirements restrict access solely to higher income households.[75]

Zoning regulations have also shaped the state's urban communities. In general, zoning rules have been motivated more by urban form and density than by fiscal requirements. Nevertheless, the imposition of density requirements or provisions restricting the height and width of multi-story towers can have the same consequences as suburban attempts at enforcing community standards—some lower cost housing solutions are precluded.[76]

Low-cost housing requires builders to economize through greater building density and smaller room sizes. So land-use requirements that restrict the maximum number of units on a site or require minimum lot sizes or minimum floor space for new construction effectively prevent the construction of unsubsidized housing that is affordable to households of low and moderate income. Estimates of the impact of these regulations on the cost of housing construction are imprecise, although builders blame costly regulations for preventing them from constructing more low-cost housing.[77]

The importance of zoning restrictions in limiting the supply of housing differs from community to community. If the state is to take the lead in pressing for the development of more affordable housing, it should play a role in encouraging localities to pay greater attention to the impact of zoning requirements on the cost of constructing housing. One way to do so would be to mandate localities to conduct explicit analysis of the cost implications of zoning requirements before new proposals are approved. This would force decision makers to confront the cost implications of zoning requirements explicitly. A second way would be to encourage negotiations between localities and developers over land-use requirements.

Estimating the cost implications of zoning policies will not guarantee that the suburbs are opened to low- and moderate-income residents. Fair-housing advocates have taken a more activist position and view the use of the courts as a possible wedge to open the suburbs.[78] Others argue that the danger of judicial intervention requires a legislative agreement on the placement of low- and moderate-income housing. The New York State Legislature has considered enacting legislation that would mandate the creation of affordable housing across the state.[79] Although these legislative efforts are well-meaning responses to the affordable housing problem, they are unlikely to be successful. While local officials may recognize the need for more affordable housing in New York, this is not the same as agreeing upon its placement.[80] It is difficult to imagine a group of state legislators purposefully precluding their jurisdictions from exercising local control over "neighborhood character."

A different approach might be to offer a carrot, rather than a stick. The state can increase allocations of intergovernmental aid or provide preferential tax treatment to local jurisdictions that adapt their building and zoning codes to allow the development of low- and moderate-income housing. Such aid could compensate localities for infrastructure and public service costs that would accompany new development (particularly in those cases where properties might be exempt from property taxes).

Building Construction Regulations

The regulation of construction activity has long been a prerogative of local governments, although passage of a statewide building and fire code in 1984 established a quality floor for all local jurisdictions. Building codes are aimed at protecting structures and inhabitants from fire danger and the hazards of shoddy construction. They provide assurances to both the building owner and the lender that some established minimum safety and quality level has been met.

These standards can be reached by mandating the use of certain construction techniques, mandating specific building materials, or by specifying certain performance standards. All approaches impose some costs on the building industry. Minimum standards requirements preclude the building industry from participating in the low-quality end of the market, even if there is consumer demand for lower quality—hence, lower priced—units. The promulgation of construction techniques and materials also reduces the returns to innovation. Cost savings from new materials and technologies cannot be realized unless they conform to code. In jurisdictions that enforce building codes, building costs are undoubtedly higher than they otherwise would be.

Building codes also affect the efficiency of the building industry in two less obvious ways. First, verification of builders' adherence to codes requires building inspection and plan approval. This is true for both performance and material standards. Verification can cause costly time delays for builders, thereby adding appreciably to the financing costs of a project. The opportunity costs of approval delay will often exceed the direct costs of fees and permits associated with pursuing development. A recent blue ribbon panel, appointed by the Mayor of the City of New York, pointed to delays in permit approvals as among the most costly, avoidable delays in the approval process.[81] Permissible delays under the City's land-use review procedures can extend up to 215 days! At a minimum, the state should consider ways to speed the verification process for performance standards.

Local building codes can also be costly to builders who operate in multiple jurisdictions because dissimilar ordinances deny them the opportunity to take advantage of economies of scale in operation. This problem still exists potentially in New York State, although the state has made significant strides in reducing the potential of across-jurisdiction code differentials. The New York State Uniform Fire Prevention Code currently mandates a statewide minimum standard of building construction, although local governments can supplement the statewide standards.

Whether the advantages of standardization outweigh the choking off of affordable housing supply is questionable. The existing code serves as a regulatory floor for all housing construction in the state. Although the uniform code permits local add-ons, it does not allow localities to administer a less stringent code. Conceivably, code requirements are set above the "appropriate" minimum standards that hold for all localities. Low-density rural areas are required to meet safety standards above those appropriate for their location. Similarly, there are individuals within the state who would prefer levels of new housing services well below that which is permitted by code to their existing housing conditions. As an example, consider the homeless. A wide range of quality levels would be preferable to existing conditions, yet a minimum quality level, far above these conditions, is mandated.

Additional flexibility could be added to the uniform code by permitting localities to make it less restrictive. For instance, a relaxation in high building standards would make it easier and less expensive to construct new housing. However, this housing is likely to be less durable and require higher maintenance expenditures in the future. Whatever the tradeoffs, a process ·should be established whereby a locality could consider loosening the local construction code, but only after careful scrutiny of the community-wide health and safety impacts. Given the severe shortage of affordable housing within the state, this option is worth examining.

Building Maintenance Requirements

Building maintenance requirements are mandated under the Uniform Fire Prevention and Building Code, with additional requirements specified in the Multiple Residence law. The evaluation of maintenance codes raises issues similar to the analysis of building codes. Underlying this evaluation is the trade-off between higher levels of building quality versus increased building and maintenance costs.

Just as building codes influence the quality of new construction, housing maintenance codes affect the quality of the existing stock. In the short term, maintenance requirements are more important for influencing state housing conditions. The existing stock of housing is much larger than new additions to the stock; on average less than one percent of the existing stock in New York State is replaced each year.[82] Further, maintenance codes affect structures that, for the most part, are occupied. In contrast, building codes are binding prior to occupancy.

Whether maintenance codes can improve the condition of existing housing depends upon the factors that lead landlords to under-invest in their properties. If the housing market is competitive, as most economists believe, under-investment in building maintenance is a rational response of profit-maximizing landlords to the prospect of uncertain increases in future rental income. Requirements that a structure be maintained at regulated quality levels are likely to be disregarded when maintenance expenditures turn the project into an inviable economic enterprise. Attempts to upgrade the housing stock through increased enforcement of building codes are likely to fail. Stricter maintenance requirements would only result in increased property abandonment as landlords walk away from non-economic properties.

On the other hand, if landlords are earning excess profits, mandates for quality improvements will get translated into increased building maintenance. Under these conditions, regulations concerning maintenance quality are much more likely to be successful.

Whatever the reasons for the landlord's behavior, the number of outstanding code violations is staggering and would impose a significant burden upon local units of government seeking to enforce the law. In 1985, New York City code inspectors conducted over 380,000 inspections and filed more than 600,000 violations. Violations in other communities are not as extensive because a greater percentage of the housing stock is occupied by owners, and the likelihood is smaller that the inspection process would be activated by a formal complaint (homeowners are both more likely to take care of their own homes and less likely than renters to complain to enforcement agents about housing conditions). Nevertheless, a successful maintenance enforcement program can play an important role in upgrading and maintaining neighborhood quality.

As long as there is a shortage of affordable housing and the costs of new construction exceed the cost of maintaining the existing stock, preserving as many standard housing units as possible is desirable. Efforts aimed at maintaining or upgrading existing housing quality, along with efforts to reduce housing abandonment, which often leads to the removal of habitable units from the existing stock, are to be encouraged. This strategy may be particularly useful in marginal neighborhoods, where perceptions of whether residents are maintaining housing quality can still affect the investment decisions of neighbors.

Environmental Quality and Historic Preservation Regulations

Environmental impact statements mandated by the State Environmental Quality Review Act can create significant obstacles to the development of affordable housing. Impact statements require significant expenditures of time and money to prepare. Additionally, they have become a favorite delay technique for groups that oppose development, through extensive court challenges. The state can maintain its commitment to both environmental quality and affordable housing by streamlining the review process.

Similarly, projects that involve developing historic structures must also be reviewed. Here too, significant delays can be encountered. Time delays can add appreciably to the financing costs of developing housing. Progress can be made in streamlining these review processes to ease the development of affordable housing.

Summary

This section has examined regulatory and subsidy approaches for reducing the cost of producing housing. Reducing the cost of constructing housing is highly desirable, however, some major impediments stand in the way of pursuing this strategy. Not everyone shares the goal of making housing more affordable. Some communities view the construction of low-cost housing as a threat to existing property values. Building trade and labor groups view the introduction of new, low-cost technologies as threatening. If lower housing prices come at the expense of housing quality, some may feel this to be an unsuitable tradeoff.

Secondly, provisions that would permit the construction of lower cost housing can only be instituted at the expense of other goals. Just as budget allocations for housing subsidies reduce the state's opportunities to conduct other programs, changes in regulatory requirements also have opportunity costs. To the extent that existing regulations contribute to the health and well-being of the state's residents, decisions about regulatory changes may require tradeoffs between housing costs and these outcomes. To the extent that the existing regulatory requirements are inefficient or unnecessary, regulatory changes can be made with minimal impact.

Rent Control Policy Options

Despite their low standing in the analytic community, rent regulations retain their widespread political appeal. Both the legislature and the Governor have suggested reforms that have moved the system in the direction of increased regulation. The prognosis for imminent reform of the existing system is poor because of the strength of the tenant movement and elected officials' fear of alienating their electorate in the next election.

Nevertheless, the turn of the century is far enough away that some political leaders may be willing to take positions that would reduce the regulatory environment of the future. Although the principle is easier to state than it is to effectuate, the direction of its intent is clear—it is desirable to move toward less-regulated housing markets while, at the same time, safeguarding existing tenants. A number of policy proposals which can help achieve this goal are discussed below.

Any change from the existing system is likely to be met by fervent opposition from either landlords or tenants. Nevertheless, the existing problems in controlled housing markets require attention. Three possible policy options that would move existing regulated markets to a less-regulated level are offered for consideration.

Vacancy Decontrol

Vacancy decontrol would provide a mechanism for a gradual transition to a less-regulated housing market. New York City briefly experimented with vacancy decontrol in 1971, but rapidly rising rents in the decontrolled sector led the state legislature to pass the Emergency Tenant Protection Act (ETPA) of 1974. The ETPA placed formerly decontrolled, vacated apartments under the rent stabilization laws. Since 1974, the legislature has renewed ETPA each time the legislation has lapsed.

The elegance of vacancy decontrol is that it facilitates a transition to a more freely functioning housing market without imposing losses on existing tenants. Each unit added to the decontrolled stock reduces the administrative burden on DHCR, increases the cash flow of building owners, permits greater maintenance, and loosens the existing tight housing market. By the year 2000, the number of potential additions to the unregulated stock through decontrol is large. In 1984, the median age of males in the 220,000 units under Rent Control was 63.2; for females it was 68.4.[83] There is a good chance that a large number of these units will be vacated over the next two decades.

A move toward decontrol must be accompanied by certain tenant safeguards. These safeguards, including harsh, enforceable penalties, should protect existing tenants from unscrupulous landlords. Decontrolled apartments in prime areas can rent at many times the controlled rent, so the incentives to encourage tenants to vacate their lease are strong. Tenants must be assured of freedom from landlord harassment if vacancy decontrol is to be successful. Clear and fair guidelines also must be established for tenant succession. Fragile family structures, non-traditional living arrangements, and the lack of housing opportunity have resulted in a large number of potential claimants to the rights of controlled apartments. Care must be taken to deal with this highly charged issue in an equitable manner. Further, the administrative and legal complexities of this process must not be underestimated.

A highly visible and controversial consequence of gradual decontrol will be the wide variations in rents charged for similar apartments, perhaps in the same building. This outcome need not be viewed with alarm. While many are likely to view such situations to be inequitable, they may also be seen as a necessary consequence of moving to a healthier housing market. First, this arrangement will be temporary and its impact mitigated as more and more units join the unregulated stock. Second, tenants demonstrably are willingly paying the higher rents to live in those deregulated units, so our sense of their misfortune should be tempered.

The politics accompanying the repeal of vacancy decontrol suggest that the value of efficiency gains does not hold much sway in Albany, relative to the standing of existing tenant groups. The impact of the arguments advanced by those seeking to decontrol rents is reduced further when it is pointed out that the revenues from rental increases flow directly to owners.

The value of vacancy decontrol to landlords is a function of how quickly decontrol occurs and the difference between regulated and deregulated rents (a difference that should decline as the deregulated stock grows and new units are brought into the system). The increased income stream can be viewed as a windfall transfer to landlords if the change in governmental policy was unanticipated and the landlords' original purchase price of the building reflected its controlled status. Although decontrol will result in a number of desirable impacts, including providing better price allocational signals, inducing increased maintenance behavior, and perhaps inducing increased future supply, the attendant distributional consequences will be difficult to defend.

Purchasing Vacancy Decontrol

One proposal to mitigate the redistribution towards building owners is to extract a payment from landlords when an apartment is vacated and moves from controlled to decontrolled status. The Rent Stabilization Association of New York (RSA), representing building owners of stabilized apartments, supports such a plan with the proceeds going to a Housing Trust Fund. The Trust Fund could then be used to construct and rehabilitate more housing for the poor. The proposal has been examined by others and rejected in part because RSA's proposed buy-out fee is small relative to the gain that landlords would realize.[84]

The size of the buy-out fee is an important issue and must be resolved if this proposal is to proceed. The key to this proposal is that it makes the relationship between rent regulations and the value of the asset explicit. This interrelationship can be exploited further by expanding the reach of the proposal.[85]

Changes in rent regulation create changes in asset value. Current law and subsequent interpretive rulings by the courts have essentially stripped building owners of their property rights. The power to set contract rents and to evict and select renters has been superceded by the rights of tenants. But these tenant rights provide no vehicle for the housing market to respond to changes in demand and supply.

Presently, tenant rights are only good as long as the tenant occupies a specific apartment. The result is lock-in. Tenants wanting to move because their circumstances have changed have nowhere to go. Landlords are shackled with unhappy tenants, some living in apartments but preferring to live elsewhere, while rent rolls are insufficient to cover necessary maintenance. This creates a double whammy. Tenants suffer because the property right is worth less to them than the rent money they save. Owners suffer because the rents they collect are well below what other tenants would be willing to pay, leading to a reduction in the levels of building maintenance and profits. Everybody suffers because the housing stock deteriorates and mobility is restricted.

One way out of the rent control quagmire is to transfer the full property rights to regulated apartments to tenants. Tenants interested in moving could sell their property rights back to the building owner, who could then charge market rents for the unit. Those tenants who did not want to sell would maintain their rent regulated status for as long as they occupied the apartment. Negotiated sales could occur at any time prior to when the tenant vacates the apartment.

Tenants who sell their property right realize a windfall that would not otherwise occur. These tenant windfalls can be used to help alleviate the shortage of low cost housing in New York City. By taxing tenant windfalls, an appreciable amount of money could be raised for an affordable housing trust fund.

If no sale was arranged by the time the apartment was vacated, property rights would be transferred back to the owners. In those cases, landlords would realize a windfall. In exchange for this windfall, landlords would also be expected to pay into a trust fund to create affordable housing. In contrast to rent control, this affordable housing trust fund could be used to help only those households least able to afford adequate housing.

A number of points should be kept in mind when considering these proposals. First, it is desirable to move towards a less regulated system. Second, the reclassification of previously controlled apartments creates value—value that has at least three potential claimants—building owners, renters, and the jurisdiction. Third, the city can accomplish other desirable housing goals by sharing in the value creation accompanying decontrol.

Control Insurance

A major criticism of rent regulations is that they discourage suppliers of housing services from constructing new housing. If suppliers are concerned that future governmental regulations will restrict the rental flow from new additions to the stock, uncertainty results and a disincentive is created. Even if suppliers merely hold some expectation of future controls, new housing supply gets choked off.

Past experience with New York's rent regulation system gives housing suppliers some cause for skepticism about the stability of existing laws. The rent-regulation system has pursued a meandering course to reach its present complex structure of laws. Rent regulations were originally created as a temporary, post-war relief measure to counter the rising rent levels of a tight housing market about to be further saturated by the return of World War II veterans. Today, they have evolved into what seems to be a permanent feature of New York City's housing markets.

The administration of the rent guidelines has also resulted in uncertainty for suppliers. Consider the changing classes of properties that are subject to rent control. Apartments that were once subject to controls become decontrolled under the vacancy decontrol measure of 1971, and then, only 3 years later, covered by rent stabilization under the Emergency

Tenant Protection Act of 1974. Similarly, the treatment and classification of new construction has changed and shifted, depending upon whether tenant or landlord interests are in the ascendence. In other words, if the specter of government involvement has a chilling effect, there has been ample opportunity for the housing industry to have been discouraged.

The market failure in this instance is one of expectations. Profit-oriented developers consider future rental values when making investment decisions. Projects that are subject to rent control will undergo a different scrutiny from those that are able to collect market-determined rents. If investors believe that changes in governmental policy are likely to reduce future returns, less housing will be constructed than would otherwise be the case.

The government can play a useful role in these situations by influencing expectations. One way to do so would be to provide an assurance to developers that their projects will maintain the existing regulated status for the period of ownership. Thus, if a developer was to build housing that was not subject to control, the government would provide "insurance" that the building would retain that status. A change in control status would result in a claim against the policy, i.e., the developer would be compensated for the capitalized loss of rental stream. Thus, the building owner would be compensated for any governmental taking.

8

Housing New York State's Elderly Population*

Introduction

Not too many years ago, the dominant public perception of the elderly population was of a group in deserving need. The world of aging was seen through the filters of what have been called "compassionate stereotypes," which held that most of the aged were involuntarily deprived—poor, frail, ill-housed, unable to keep up with inflation, and so forth. These perceptions were reinforced by the political rhetoric of public officials, candidates for office, and leaders of age-based organizations. In the last few years, however, many academic studies, government reports, and op-ed pieces in the *New York Times* and other national newspapers have challenged the stereotype. Indeed, for many people in the informed electorate (though polls show not in the public at large), an opposite stereotype may have taken hold. As might be expected, there is a degree of truth in both perspectives.

Any analysis of how elderly residents of New York State will be housed in the year 2000 must begin with an accurate portrayal of their current living situations. As shall be seen below, the great majority of aged New Yorkers (i.e., those 65 and older) are able to live independently in homes and apartments they like and where they prefer to remain. Moreover, there are reasons to believe there will be improvements in the housing stock occupied by the elderly in New York through the rest of this century.

However, significant numbers of senior citizens do face housing-related hardships, which may combine deficits in economic well being, physical conditions of homes and apartments, or functional limitations among the elderly themselves. While some sources of such disadvantage will continue to decline in importance, others are likely to increase in the decades to come. The most important of the latter will be the explosive growth in the number of "old-old" New Yorkers, who are the most likely to face financial and physical difficulties.

---

*This chapter was authored by Bruce Jacobs.

Undoubtedly, the private sector will continue to play the dominant role in providing housing options for the elderly in this state. Yet government policies have had an important impact on the living situations of many older New Yorkers, and decisions at all levels of government will affect the kinds of housing alternatives from which they must choose (as well as their prices). The housing needs of the aged will primarily be defined by their preferences and their capabilities. Although several housing options will be considered in this report, we should be cautious in prescribing programs, either for long-range government planning or in anticipation of the development of private sector alternatives.

Independent Living for Older New Yorkers

The dominant trend in the housing situation of America's elderly population since the Second World War has been the increasing ability to maintain their own households. Fully 81 percent of those 65 years and older in New York are household heads or their spouses.[86] In decades past, this figure was substantially lower. By 1980, elderly New Yorkers headed 21 percent of all households, even though they represent only 11 percent of the state's population.

Various reasons have been offered to explain this high degree of independent living. Perhaps most important among them is that older New Yorkers can now afford to head their own households (albeit at great expense in some cases). Virtually all survey data reveal, moreover, that the elderly prefer to live in their own housing units, wanting neither to live in the homes of other family members nor to join with unrelated (aged or nonaged) people in new households. In fact, only 11 percent of those 65 or older live in other family members' houses, and about one percent are in households whose heads are not related to them. The remaining six percent of New York's elderly live in what the Census Bureau calls "group quarters."[87] Nearly 90 percent are in nursing homes and mental hospitals.

There are important differences in the degree to which various elderly demographic groups can live independently. Both age and marital status have significant statistical effects on the ability to maintain a household. Table 19 shows that as elderly New Yorkers grow older they are less likely to head households, with barely half of those who are 85 or older able to do so. This is the fastest growing age group in New York (as well as the rest of the nation), and in years to come it will present significant challenges to New York State's policy makers.

While 95 percent of married people head households, just over two-thirds of unmarried (mostly widowed) New Yorkers do so. There are at

TABLE 19

PERCENTAGE OF ELDERLY PERSONS LIVING AS HOUSEHOLD HEADS OR THEIR SPOUSES, BY AGE AND MARITAL STATUS

Marital Status

AGE	Married	Unmarried	All
65 - 69	97%	78%	90%
70 - 74	96	76	87
75 - 79	96	73	82
80 - 84	91	60	69
85 +	81	44	51
All	95%	68%	81%

SOURCE: Tabulated from the New York State sample, 1980 PUMS data.

least three reasons why unmarried people are less likely to be household heads. First, unmarried people are disproportionately in advanced old age. Twenty-nine percent of older married persons are age 75 or more, compared with 52 percent of those who are not married. Being among the old-old, in turn, is correlated with having low income. Fewer than one quarter of those age 65 to 69 have household incomes less than 150 percent of the federal government's poverty line. The prevalence of such low income rises steadily with age, with nearly one-half of the oldest old (85 or older) in this category.[88] Low income obviously constrains a person's ability to live independently and cover the various costs associated with housing. It also, however, may increase the challenge of physical independence in old age.

While most older people have chronic conditions of various types, only a minority have conditions so serious that they need the help of other people to get by.[89] Gerontologists have categorized the need for human assistance at three general levels. The least serious (in the sense of how much help is needed) are "instrumental activities of daily living" (e.g., cleaning house). The next level is dependence on others for mobility (e.g., getting out of a chair or climbing stairs). The most fundamental threat to independent living occurs when a person needs assistance in an "activity of daily living" (ADL), which can include bathing, dressing, toileting, or feeding, among others.[90]

There are essentially three ways in which people with ADL problems have obtained help. The bulk of such services is provided informally by spouses or, in fewer cases, by other family members.[91] A second source of human assistance is the purchase of formal care services in the community. Although there is a growing market for such services, relatively few of those who need them choose to (or can afford to) pay for them. (New York State has taken the lead in providing formal services using Medicaid funds. However, only a modest portion of the funds needed for complete coverage is available, and to qualify for Medicaid very stringent income and asset eligibility criteria must be met.)

The principal method for obtaining formal services for those dependent in personal care is entry into a nursing home or a related institution. This step is considered to be the least desirable alternative for the vast majority of those who need extensive help. In fact, only a minority of people so afflicted are institutionalized.

Other research has shown that as people age into their oldest years, and as they begin to live without spouses, the probability of being dependent in personal care grows sharply,[92] as does the probability of being in institutions.[93] Table 20 documents the latter relationship as it occurs in New York. Although only six percent of people age 65 or older live in nursing homes, mental hospitals, or other group quarters, the probability of not living in the community varies greatly by age and marital status. While virtually no married persons between the ages of 65 and 69 are in group quarters, almost three in ten single persons aged 85 or over are so situated. The combination of low income, increased probability of need for human assistance in important areas of physical functioning, and the probable absence of available informal services from a spouse (fewer than 20 percent are married) seriously threatens the ability of the oldest old to live independently in the community. (Recall, however, that just over half still head their own households.)

The various effects of very old age and (in most cases) widowhood will be of central importance to the housing of older New Yorkers in the decades to come. These demographic characteristics cannot be manipulated through public policy intervention. Without major changes in public and private financing of nursing home care, if rates of dependence and institutionalization continue on their present course, there will be important implications for state (and local) outlays through the Medicaid program. The pressures on families for informal care and financial assistance also will grow accordingly. Absent unanticipated changes in

TABLE 20

**PERCENTAGE OF ELDERLY PERSONS NOT LIVING IN THE COMMUNITY,
BY AGE AND MARITAL STATUS**

	Marital Status		
AGE	Married	Unmarried	All
65 - 69	0%*	4%	2%
70 - 74	1	6	3
75 - 79	1	8	5
80 - 84	4	15	12
85+	11	29	26
All	1%	11%	6%

*Rounded to nearest percentage.
SOURCE: Tabulated from the New York State sample, 1980 PUMS data.

morbidity rates and family structures, the nursing home population in New York State is expected to rise substantially during the remainder of this century.

A Profile of Elderly Households in New York

Approximately 1.3 million New York households are headed by someone age 65 or older, accounting for about one-fifth of the state's households. While this significant presence in the housing stock mirrors the figure for the United States, New York differs from the national pattern in one important respect—housing tenure. In the United States, just under three-quarters of all older householders are homeowners. In New York, however, there is an even split between homeowners and renters.

Table 21 documents the geographic distribution of elderly households and regional rates of home ownership. Most striking is the fact that nearly three-quarters of aged household heads in New York City are renters. Since the city has almost half of all elderly households in the state, it lowers drastically the overall rate of home ownership. Excepting these

TABLE 21

GEOGRAPHIC LOCATION AND TENURE OF ELDERLY HOUSEHOLDS

REGION	Total	Owners	Renters	% Owners
BUFFALO	98,100	65,400	32,700	67%
ROCHESTER	66,100	43,800	22,300	66
SYRACUSE	81,200	56,100	25,100	69
SOUTHERN TIER	86,800	65,100	21,700	75
UPPER HUDSON	75,000	47,000	28,000	63
NORTH COUNTRY	44,400	33,300	11,100	75
MID HUDSON	52,600	36,900	15,700	70
NEW YORK CITY	617,000	170,400	446,600	27
NORTHERN NYC SUBURBS	78,900	43,200	35,700	55
LONG ISLAND	132,300	106,200	26,100	80
NEW YORK STATE	1,332,400	667,400	665,000	50%

SOURCE: Tabulated from the New York State sample, 1980 PUMS data.

617,000 units, about two-thirds of New York State's units are owned. Nevertheless, just over one-quarter of all older homeowners in the state live in New York City.

Adding the suburban regions adjacent to New York City, a picture of downstate quantitative dominance emerges. New York, its northern suburbs, and Long Island collectively account for 62 percent of all elderly households, including nearly half of owners and just over three-quarters of renters. Table 22 fleshes out the percentage distribution by tenure across the state's regions.

It has long been noted among gerontologists that the aged are at least as heterogeneous as the population of those under the age of 65. Three key characteristics divide the elderly into groups with quite different housing situations in New York (and in the nation). As discussed above, age and marital status have substantial statistical effects on the probability of living independently. Housing tenure of those in the community is another key dimension, although it is related to some extent to the others. While 53

TABLE 22

GEOGRAPHIC DISTRIBUTION OF ELDERLY HOUSEHOLDS

REGION	% of all elderly Households	% of elderly Owners	% of elderly Renters
BUFFALO	7%	10%	5%
ROCHESTER	5	7	3
SYRACUSE	6	8	4
SOUTHERN TIER	7	10	3
UPPER HUDSON	6	7	4
NORTH COUNTRY	3	5	2
MID HUDSON	4	6	2
NEW YORK CITY	46	26	67
NORTHERN NYC SUBURBS	6	7	5
LONG ISLAND	10	16	4
NEW YORK STATE	100%	102%*	99%*

*Not equal to 100% because of rounding
SOURCE: Tabulated from the New York State sample, 1980 PUMS data.

percent of elderly owners are not married, for example, fully 69 percent of renters live without a mate.

These three variables are strongly related to the economic well being of the aged. Overall, just over one-third of elderly family and individual households have before-tax cash incomes that are below 150 percent of the federal government's poverty line.[94] Low-income rates are much higher, however, for renters (46 percent), unmarried householders (48 percent), and those aged 75 years or older (43 percent) than for owners, married heads, and the young old (24 percent, 17 percent, and 30 percent, respectively). Of all low-income householders, nearly four-fifths are single, two-thirds renters, and one-half aged 75 or older. Table 23 displays the combined effects of these three factors on the likelihood of having very low incomes.

Perhaps surprisingly, the prevalence of low incomes does not vary much across New York State. The North Country region has the only rate

TABLE 23

PERCENTAGE OF ELDERLY HOUSEHOLDS WITH LOW INCOME,*
BY MARITAL STATUS, AGE, AND TENURE

	MARRIED		UNMARRIED	
AGE	Owners	Renters	Owners	Renters
65 - 69	11%	19%	28%	50%
70 - 74	14	22	36	52
75 - 79	15	26	38	60
80 - 84	24	28	42	63
85+	31	36	42	62

*Income less than 150% of the poverty line.
SOURCE: Tabulated from the New York State sample, 1980 PUMS data.

above 52 percent. Both of New York City's suburban regions have rates below 40 percent. All other areas are closely bunched in between.

Quality of the Elderly's Housing[95]

The National Housing Act of 1949 set forth the goal of a "decent home in a suitable living environment" for every American. The 1981 White House Conference on Aging renewed this call for all aged persons. Many believe, however, that the goal has been largely unmet. When the Louis Harris organization asked a national sample of adult Americans whether they felt that poor housing was a "very serious problem" for those aged 65 or more, fully 43 percent said yes.[96]

How adequate are the structures in which New York State's elderly population lives? There are two approaches one might take in answering this question. One is to measure the characteristics of homes and apartments objectively and compare them with professional standards of adequacy. The second is to assess what the elderly think and do about their housing as they make their own judgments. Previous research has shown that there can be a significant difference between objective housing "needs" as measured by housing analysts and the subjective preferences of the elderly regarding their housing situations.[97]

One problem that has plagued housing researchers is that there is no single valid standard against which to measure whether a structure is a decent home. In addition to the impact of widely varying values and cultures, measurement efforts have been made difficult by the fact that societal standards change over time. What is considered acceptable housing in one decade may be considered inadequate in the next. Moreover, most professional definitions of adequacy are not directly linked with serious physical or psychological hazards that could add validity to the measurement of housing quality.

One standard of adequacy that illustrates these concerns is whether there is enough space in a housing unit. The concept of overcrowding has undergone substantial change in the last few decades. In the 1940 and 1950 U.S. Censuses of Housing, densities exceeding two persons per room defined overcrowding. This standard was dropped to 1.5 in 1960 and 1970. For 1980, the Census Bureau reported the percentage of housing units with more than one person per room. This increasing standard is not based on the measured impact of overcrowding on residents. Rather, it is a recognition of the fact that social norms have changed over time.

Regardless of the import of overcrowding as currently measured, it is clear that the elderly households of New York State (as in the nation as a whole) do not suffer from this housing inadequacy. Fewer than one in a hundred such units have less than one room per person. Only a fifth have less than two rooms. In fact, older New York householders have half again as much space per person on average as those under the age of 65 (3.1 vs. 2.1 rooms). This pattern holds true for owners (3.6 vs. 2.3) and nearly so for renters (2.6 vs. 2.0).

The simple reason elderly households have so much space per person is that they do not have relatives or other people living with them. About 80 percent of older householders live by themselves or only with their spouses. This pattern holds true even in households headed by the old-old. (Recall, however, that smaller portions of this population actually head households.)

Not withstanding the fact that any objective measure of satisfactory housing conditions must be arbitrary, it is possible to describe the adequacy of structures across New York State by noting the absence of certain basic facilities: complete plumbing; heating not dependent on room heaters, stoves, fireplaces, etc.; and exclusive use of complete kitchen facilities.[98] Overall, elderly headed housing units are slightly less likely to be without one of these features than younger households (8.6 percent vs. 9.8 percent). This is the case for both owners (8.1 percent vs. 8.4 percent) and renters (8.9 percent vs. 11.5 percent).

Table 24 lists the percentage of inadequate units in each of the state's

TABLE 24

PERCENTAGE OF ELDERLY-HEADED HOUSING UNITS
THAT ARE INADEQUATE,*
BY REGION AND TENURE

REGION	Owners	Renters	All Units
BUFFALO	10%	15%	12%
ROCHESTER	7	9	7
SYRACUSE	11	9	11
SOUTHERN TIER	14	26	17
UPPER HUDSON	10	22	15
NORTH COUNTRY	20	20	20
MID HUDSON	9	12	10
NEW YORK CITY	6	7	7
NORTHERN NYC SUBURBS	5	6	5
LONG ISLAND	3	2	3
NEW YORK STATE	8%	9%	9%

*Inadequacy is defined as being without working plumbing, central heating, or kitchen facilities.
SOURCE: Tabulated from the New York State sample, 1980 PUMS data.

regions. The highest rates appear in those regions without major metropolitan areas (i.e., the North Country and the Southern Tier). In locations outside of Census-defined standard metropolitan statistical areas, just over 17 percent of elderly headed housing units are deficient in either plumbing, heating, or kitchen facilities. Yet, these rural areas only contain a fifth of New York's inadequate homes. New York City, which has one of the lowest rates of inadequacy, has three-eighths of all such units in the State. Thus, while houses in less densely populated areas are more likely to be inadequate, inadequate units are not primarily located in rural areas. It is worthy to note that Long Island has the lowest prevalence of substandard housing. In part, this reflects the fact that it has the youngest housing stock in the state (a median age of just under thirty years, the only region less than forty). The aging of suburbia should lower rates of housing inadequacy in the future as more of the state's elderly are located in homes constructed after World War II.

As might be expected, families with low incomes are more likely to have substandard housing. The inadequacy rate for those with incomes less than 150 percent of the poverty line, however, is only three percent higher than for all elderly households. In contrast, low-income nonelderly households are six percent more likely to have deficient units than are all younger households. Inadequacy rates for the low-income aged are also lower than for other low-income households (12 percent vs. 16 percent). While there are a nontrivial number of older families and individuals in substandard units, the problem of housing quality is not simply a function of the householder's old age or low income. This is true, in part, because aged widows often experience a deterioration in income not reflected in their house's condition.

How the Elderly Assess Their Housing

In contrast to what many in the public believe, the great majority of elderly persons across the nation enjoy their housing situations, do not think their housing is inadequate, and do not want to move. In the 1981 Harris poll, only five percent of those aged 65 or older said that poor housing was a serious problem for them personally (compared with seven percent of younger respondents). Of the variety of concerns raised in interviews with the elderly (e.g., income, health, crime), housing ranked dead last, as it had in a similar 1974 survey.[99] (In a 1986 national survey of the aged, Harris dropped the question of housing problems entirely.[100])

A 1975 study of elderly homeowners allowed researchers to compare directly what housing specialists identified as needs for home repair with what the elderly thought were serious problems in their houses. In all types of possible repairs (from roofs and gutters to windows, floors, and foundations), older homeowners said there was less need than did housing specialists who had inspected their homes.[101] In short, elderly homeowners were more satisfied with the adequacy of their houses than were the objective experts.

One must be cautious in interpreting these and other survey results suggesting a disparity between the elderly's subjective assessment of their housing and what experts or the public believe are the needs of the elderly. Various psychological and sociological explanations have been offered to account for these and similar differences.[102] Also, in cases of a severe problem (e.g., a staircase about to collapse), we must recognize a serious housing inadequacy regardless of what an elderly resident says or believes. A nontrivial percentage of the imputed need for better housing, however, may be neither reflective of a direct threat to health or safety nor a major source of concern for elderly households themselves.[103]

Ironically, some planners have defined the major problem of elderly housing as one of too much space. In their view, many of the aged are "overhoused," living in units with empty bedrooms and other unused space (especially in owner-occupied homes). It would be more efficient for them (and society) if they moved to smaller units, with better use of space and lower upkeep and utilities costs. Relinquishing their "empty nests," they would allow younger families to buy homes not now available in a very tough housing market.

The major shortcoming of this perspective is that it runs afoul of the notion of consumer sovereignty. Most of the elderly do not themselves think they have too much unused space in their houses. Nearly three-quarters of elderly homeowners interviewed in one study said the size of their house was just right.[104] Among the reasons given for this opinion was that older owners want some place to put up their children and other family when they visit.

More generally, a majority of the elderly have been living where they are for quite a long time (a median of 25 years for owners and 10 years for renters in New York State) and profess little reason to leave their homes. Yet, one might also argue that some of the elderly do not perceive or do not have alternative housing options that would be preferred by them.[105] Survey data on older peoples' attachment to their current housing units are so consistent, however, that even those analysts who question the advisability of many living arrangements recognize that these findings cannot be ignored.[106]

Whatever the reason for staying in their houses, older people have not shown much desire to move. From 1983 to 1984, for example, only 4.6 percent of those 65 or older moved, compared to a rate of 17.3 percent for all Americans.[107] New York State's older population, however, has shown much higher than average propensities to move out of state than have others in the country. In the latter half of the 1960s, New Yorkers accounted for 13.8 percent of all interstate migration of the aged and had by far the greatest number of movers to the sunbelt. Yet, even this high level of migration over a five-year period represented only 5.5 percent of New York's 1970 population aged 65 or older.[108] A similar pattern held in the late 1970s. Although those aged 55 or older accounted for about a quarter of the state's net population loss through migration to the sunbelt, the total number of these migrants was about five percent of the 1980 population similarly aged. During the same period, seven percent of those aged 65 or older moved to another state.[109]

There is as yet no valid theory of elderly migration. Rather, there have been more or less successful attempts to focus on several kinds of factors at work when older people move. Mobility rates, for example, are lowest among the old-old. Most (85 percent) New Yorkers who move to Florida are below the age of 75, and thus are more likely to have higher incomes and intact marriages. For these people, moving represents a desirable opportunity. For others, however, mobility may be a distasteful necessity. Changing economic or health status may force elderly New Yorkers to abandon their long-term residences.

Regardless of the reasons for moving, most important in this context is the fact that relatively few aged New Yorkers actually pick up roots and change their housing. To envision a housing pattern quite different from today's would implicitly require the elderly to have much different preferences in the future, to have much greater incomes and assets allowing them to choose alternative housing not affordable now, or to have much less capacity to live independently where they are. Each of these factors may emerge to some extent in the future. It is unlikely, however, that a revolution in the elderly's housing arrangements will take place during the rest of this century. Evaluations of the potential impact of innovative housing arrangements should be carried out in this context.

The Problem of Housing Affordability

In one sense, independent living gives ample proof that the great majority of New York State's older population can afford their housing. Indeed, the substantial increase in household headship rates among those aged 65 or older has been one measure of their improved economic condition across the country.[110] Housing analysts, however, prefer to measure the affordability of housing in relation to its impact on a family's budget.

Federal housing assistance programs require that recipients pay up to 30 percent of their household income for rent. The remainder of housing costs are considered an excess housing expense burden. The 30 percent figure is, of course, an arbitrary one. Last decade, it was 25 percent. Some analysts, in fact, now suggest that the standard might be increased to 35 percent.[111]

Using the current standard, excess rental expense burdens in New York State closely match those in the nation. Just under half (48 percent) of all older New York renters pay more than 30 percent of their incomes for housing compared with 36 percent of those under age 65. The national figures are 50 percent and 38 percent respectively.[112] While the costs of renting are, on average, lower than those of owning,[113] the much lower incomes of renters result in higher excess cost rates.

Table 25 details rates of excess housing expense burdens of both renters and owners in New York and in the U.S. (As defined by the U.S. Department of Housing and Urban Development, excess ownership costs are those greater than 40 percent of a family's income.[114]) As seen in the bottom row, the total prevalence of excess housing expense burdens in New York is higher than it is in the nation for both elderly and nonelderly households. This pattern is a function of two factors. First, the much higher prevalence of rental households in New York brings up the total rate of excess housing burdens. In addition, ownership costs in this state are higher fractions of elderly family budgets than in other states.

TABLE 25

RATES OF EXCESS HOUSING EXPENSE BURDENS* IN
NEW YORK AND IN THE U.S.
BY TENURE AND AGE

	NEW YORK STATE		UNITED STATES	
	Elderly	Non-elderly	Elderly	Non-elderly
RENTERS	48%	36%	50%	38%
OWNERS	20	10	11	8
ALL UNITS	38	26	24	20

*Excess housing expense burdens are over 30% of a renter's income and over 40% of an owner's income.
SOURCE: New York State 1980 PUMS data and national 1980 Annual Housing Survey data.

The differences between elderly and nonelderly expense burdens in New York State are substantially more than in the nation as a whole. In New York, the elderly are no more likely to be homeowners than are younger householders. This is not true for the United States overall. National rates of excess expenses are brought down because of higher ownership rates for the elderly, but this is not the case in New York.

Very high rental cost burdens suggest that New Yorkers may have changed their subjective judgments of what is an excessive expenditure for rent. On this basis, the threshold might be raised to 40 percent of income for renters as well as owners. Such a change can be interpreted either as the use of a more valid standard or as producing an underestimate of the affordability problem for renters. Elderly renters, in fact, still have higher rates of the newly defined excess housing costs than do elderly owners (34 percent vs. 20 percent). In any event, the problem of cost in the rental marketplace is clearly a serious one.

Table 26 displays the pattern of excess housing cost burdens among elderly households across New York. In general, downstate regions tend to

TABLE 26

**PERCENTAGE OF ELDERLY HOUSEHOLDS WHO SPEND MORE THAN 40%
OF THEIR INCOMES ON HOUSING**

REGION	Owners*	Renters	All Households
BUFFALO	14%	32%	22%
ROCHESTER	14	32	21
SYRACUSE	15	35	23
SOUTHERN TIER	14	36	21
UPPER HUDSON	16	28	20
NORTH COUNTRY	19	28	22
MID HUDSON	26	41	31
NEW YORK CITY	25	34	33
NORTHERN NYC SUBURBS	23	36	30
LONG ISLAND	28	43	31
NEW YORK STATE	20%	34%	29%

*Excludes cooperative apartments and condominiums.
SOURCE: Tabulated from the New York State sample, 1980 PUMS data.

have higher rates than elsewhere in the state. One exception is the average prevalence of excess cost burdens among elderly renters in New York City—a reflection of its highly regulated rental market prices.

Average yearly homeowner costs in each of the first seven regions were under $3,000 (in 1980 dollars). New York City owners paid out over $3,500. Older owners in its suburbs paid out over $4,000. As noted above, excess housing expense burdens for elderly homeowners in New York State are nearly twice as prevalent as in the nation. Like other elderly owners in the United States, however, over four-fifths (83 percent) of older New Yorkers have paid off their mortgages and own their homes free and clear. Thus the great bulk of their home ownership expenditures is for utilities, property taxes, and insurance. Table 27 documents the sub-

TABLE 27

PERCENTAGE OF ELDERLY HOMEOWNERS WHO SPEND MORE THAN 40% OF THEIR INCOMES ON UTILITIES, TAXES, AND INSURANCE

REGION	All Elderly Homeowners	Low Income* Elderly Homeowners
BUFFALO	11%	42%
ROCHESTER	11	47
SYRACUSE	12	48
SOUTHERN TIER	11	38
UPPER HUDSON	13	57
NORTH COUNTRY	17	49
MID HUDSON	22	58
NEW YORK CITY	20	81
NORTHERN NYC SUBURBS	21	93
LONG ISLAND	24	80
NEW YORK STATE	14%	60%

*Income less than 150% of the poverty line.
SOURCE: Tabulated from the New York State sample, 1980 PUMS data.

stantial burden that these costs impose on homeowners' budgets. Even excluding mortgage payments, where present, New York's older owners are still 40 percent more likely to have high housing costs than owners across the United States.

Utilities, property tax, and insurance payments make an exceptionally big dent in the budgets of low-income households, especially in the New York City area. More generally, total housing costs are often near prohibitive for elderly owners and renters in this income range (especially downstate, but also in other regions). Table 28 reveals the difficult financial circumstances in which most low-income households find themselves as they pay their housing bills.

These high housing expense burdens reflect two different patterns of change over time. First, fuel prices rose dramatically in the 1970s and were

TABLE 28

**PERCENTAGE OF LOW-INCOME* ELDERLY HOUSEHOLDS WHO SPEND MORE
THAN 40% OF THEIR INCOMES ON HOUSING**

REGION	Owners	Renters	All Low-Income Households
BUFFALO	46%	56%	52%
ROCHESTER	52	54	53
SYRACUSE	52	51	52
SOUTHERN TIER	43	55	49
UPPER HUDSON	60	42	48
NORTH COUNTRY	51	39	45
MID HUDSON	61	61	61
NEW YORK CITY	86	60	62
NORTHERN NYC SUBURBS	93	60	68
LONG ISLAND	84	61	74
NEW YORK STATE	64%	58%	60%

*Income less than 150% of the poverty line.
SOURCE: Tabulated from the New York State sample, 1980 PUMS data.

added to very substantial property tax rates already present in New York
State (especially in downstate suburbs). The second important factor is the
life cycle experience of many formerly middle-class senior citizens.
Specifically, when spouses die, widows often experience significant
declines in their incomes. Social Security benefits are reduced (most often
by one-third). Many private pensions in the past have covered only the life
of the retiree (husband) and thus cease upon the onset of widowhood.
Since the unmarried aged are substantially older than married retirees,
there is less of a chance that entry into the labor force will cushion this
income decline.

Widowhood does not produce much of a reduction of housing costs,
unless an owner chooses to move to cheaper housing (or to join another
family member's household). While there are federal and state programs
that provide some fuel expense and property tax relief for low-income
elderly households, a substantial portion of this population still must
rearrange their budgets if they are to remain living independently. The fact
that they do so is another indication of how attached they are to their
housing units. It may also be true, however, that many of those with high
expense burdens do not see (and, in fact, may not have) satisfactory
alternative housing options that are any cheaper. This consideration will
figure importantly as new living arrangements are proposed and offered in
the marketplace.

Not surprisingly, the profile of low-income elderly persons (unmarried, old-old, or renter) is strongly associated with housing affordability problems. Table 29 details the combined effects of these three
risk factors on excess housing cost burden rates. Particularly noteworthy is
the fact that unmarried elderly homeowners (especially those aged 75 or
older) have housing affordability problems approaching the high rates
among renters. As discussed in the next section, many of these single
elderly owners might be helped in meeting their housing expenses without
major public sector expenditures.

There are several caveats that should be considered when interpreting these data on housing cost burdens. Some housing expenses are not
included in the analysis—most importantly, repair and maintenance costs.
Since there are no measures of need for repair in the Census data, we have
no way of knowing how much more money might be required to assure a
safe and healthy housing environment. Despite the common notion that
old people systematically allow their homes to deteriorate, an analysis of
the Annual Housing Survey national sample found that elderly owned
homes were only one percent more likely to have serious structural
deficiencies than those owned by younger people. The analogous figure for
rental units was four percent.[115]

TABLE 29

PREVALENCE OF EXCESS HOUSING EXPENSE BURDENS[*]
FOR ELDERLY HOUSEHOLDS
BY TENURE, AGE, AND MARITAL STATUS

HOMEOWNERS

	Young Old[**]	Old Old[***]	All Owners
Married	12%	15%	13%
Unmarried	28	31	29
All Owners	18	24	20

RENTERS

	Young Old[**]	Old Old[***]	All Renters
Married	18%	21%	19%
Unmarried	39	44	41
All Renters	31	38	34

[*]Housing expenses above 40% of income.
[**]Aged 65 to 74
[***]Aged 75 or more
SOURCE: Tabulated from the New York State sample, 1980 PUMS Data.

Another caution regards the fact that rental expenses already reflect the cash subsidies provided by the federal government in housing assistance programs; the implicit subsidies in rent control and stabilization; the local option of partial homestead exemptions from property tax liabilities for low income owners; and New York City's Senior Citizens Rental Increase Exemption program, which reduces the burden of potential rent increases for the older renter by subsidizing landlords. Without these subsidies, the measured housing affordability problem would be much larger. Indeed, many aged householders would undoubtedly have to give up their homes or apartments.

On the other hand, the prevalence of high housing cost burdens is inflated to the extent that these measures do not take into account all available resources of older owners and renters. Payments from the federal home energy assistance program and food stamps, for example, are not counted in the income measure. Nor are gifts, inheritances, insurance proceeds, and other lump sums received. Property tax relief from the state's circuit breaker program also is not reflected in the calculation.

Historically, the Census Bureau has found the greatest source of underreported income to be money derived from assets (e.g., in the form of interest and dividends).[116] Since elderly people as a group are most dependent on such income, there may be a serious distorting effect in the estimation of some householder's housing expense rates. However, we have reason to believe that this effect is quite modest for most older households.

While there are no data that reliably describe the asset holdings of New Yorkers, a national study (the Survey of Income and Program Participation) gives some indication of the distribution of wealth held by various groups in the United States. It found that, while 78 percent of all elderly households have some amount of money in banks, the median amount held in 1984 was only $13,255.[117] Although the median amount owned in bonds and money market funds was $18,114, only 12 percent of the aged in the United States have such assets.

The Unused Asset—Home Equity[118]

Nationally, most older folks have the bulk of their wealth tied up in their homes. Indeed, when the value of home equity (i.e., the value of the house minus outstanding mortgage debt) is subtracted, the median-aged household in the United States is worth only $18,790.[119] By definition, the same pattern cannot be true for New York State, since half of older New Yorkers are renters.[120] Yet, New York's older homeowners are likely to have large fractions of their assets in the form of home equity. The national Retirement History Survey found that the median proportion of total wealth held as net home equity is 70 percent for all elderly homeowners and 83 percent for single women (mostly widows).[121]

Although home equity is the major asset owned by these people, it has not typically been used to finance consumption. Perhaps the most important reason is that, until recently, the only way to unlock home equity has been to sell one's home and move. The great majority of elderly owners, however, have been reluctant to do this, given the attachment to their homes. The home equity loans now frequently advertised in the media also have limited potential for the elderly, because they are amortized over a short period and require monthly payments from the owner. They impose both a financial barrier (because relatively few elderly homeowners have enough other income to make those payments) and a psychological one (because the elderly have shown a substantial reluctance to accept major debt responsibilities).

To overcome these difficulties, some innovative plans have been developed that will convert home equity into income for the elderly without forcing them to move or make monthly payments on a loan. Popularly known by the generic term "reverse annuity mortgage" (or simply "reverse mortgage"), these plans have received increasing attention in the print and electronic media. They include loans that are paid back only after the elderly move or die and sales that allow the elderly to stay in their homes for as long as they wish and are able.

There are about 30 public and private programs that now enable the aged to spend some of their equity while remaining in their homes. Among neighboring states, New Jersey, Pennsylvania, Massachusetts, and Connecticut each have such plans available. Three limited programs are operating in New York State. The Home Equity Living Plan is providing about 60 Buffalo homeowners with money to cover taxes, insurance, and minor repairs, and a small monthly annuity in exchange for ownership of their property after they die.[122] In Nassau and Suffolk Counties, the Counseling for Home Equity Conversion and Reverse Annuity Mortgage Counseling program have helped more than 300 older homeowners arrange fixed-term reverse mortgage loans with local private lenders. These loans have monthly disbursements to elderly borrowers throughout the term, which averages about seven years, at the end of which both principal and accumulated interest are due in one lump sum.[123]

Mortgage lenders have heretofore been reluctant to write fixed-term reverse mortgages in part because of the end-of-term problem. If an elderly borrower outlives the term of the loan and does not want to sell her home and pay off the loan, then the lender may have to face a default or bring legal action against the homeowner, neither of which is a palatable alternative. One solution to this dilemma would be to have an insurance instrument to spread this risk over all insured reverse mortgage loans, similar to the insurance plans for conventional mortgages. A demonstration program to test this concept was proposed by the Reagan administration in 1982, but had little support in the Congress. In 1987, however, both the House and Senate housing bills called for such a program, and the final legislation provided for a demonstration program of insurance to cover 2500 reverse mortgage loans. Lenders around the country were able to offer insured loans in late 1989.

There are a few private reverse mortgage instuments that do not have an end-of-term problem for the elderly borrower. The first of these offered to elderly homeowners was the IRMA Plan (sold by the American Homestead Company in New Jersey, Pennsylvania, and Connecticut, among other states), which provides monthly payments for as long as the borrower wants to stay in his or her home.[124] In exchange for this, however, the homeowner must give up a share of the appreciation in home value after the inception of the loan. If the older homeowner remains in her home a very long while, the loan turns out to be a good deal. However, if the loan is paid off fairly quickly, the effective rate of interest is quite high.[125] The risks of short and long lifetimes to the borrower and lender are thus analogous to those in lifetime annuity contracts sold by insurance companies (i.e., the customer wins if he or she survives into very old age).

So far, American Homestead has written about as many reverse mortgage loans as all other private lenders put together. However, the plan (and a few similar ones more recently marketed) is not available to older New York homeowners. This is because state banking law does not permit mortgage lendres to write loans with shared appreciation as a form of interest. In recent years, attempts to change this situation through legislation have failed. Whether, or when, New Yorkers will be able to borrow against their home equity while remaining at home receiving monthly payments for as long as they want and are able is unknown.[126]

Previous research has shown that home equity conversion could have a large impact on the incomes of many of the aged.[127] The subgroups of elderly homeowners who could be helped the most tend to be those who need it most. Specifically, those who need more income (i.e., the old-old and single) are the ones who will get the highest reverse mortgage payments for a given amount of home equity. This is because homeowners who are of very advanced age and alone can spread their equity over a shorter number of years, since their household life expectancies are much lower than for young-old and married owners. Even though old-old singles tend to have lower incomes, the impact of compounding interest affects their loans much less than for other borrowers seeking long-term loan disbursements.

To illustrate this pattern of the potential benefit of home equity conversion, consider the national estimates presented in Tables 30 and 31. Table 30 shows that singles in general, and low-income singles in particular, could realize the greatest percentage changes in their incomes. At the median, a single borrower could raise her income by a quarter. The median low-income single aged 75 or older could have her income raised by 58 percent.[128]

Table 31 documents the impressive impact that reverse mortgages could have on excess housing expense burden rates in the United States. The prevalence of excess burdens could be reduced by half among elderly

TABLE 30

POTENTIAL PERCENTAGE INCREASES IN INCOME FROM REVERSE
MORTGAGES, BY FAMILY STRUCTURE AND INCOME LEVEL

	Singles		Couples	
	low income*	higher income**	low income*	higher income**
Percentage Increase in income				
less than 10 %	14%	24%	26%	56%
10% to 14%	4	14	16	20
15% to 24%	12	25	23	16
25% to 32%	9	12	10	4
33% to 49%	18	14	12	3
50% or more	43	11	13	1
Total	100%	100%	100%	100%

*Income less than 150% of the poverty line.
**Income greater than or equal to 150% of the poverty line.
SOURCE: Tabulated from the 1983 Annual Housing Survey
Bruce Jacobs, "The National Potential of Home Equity Conversion"

singles and couples.[129] For singles and those over 75, the reduction would be greater. (Recall, however, that the size of the problem of housing affordability among New York's elderly homeowners is nearly twice as great to begin with.)

The single most frequent use to which home equity conversion has been put has been to reduce the burden of property taxes. In California, Oregon, and a few other states, elderly homeowners can defer payment of their property taxes until their death or the sale of their home. The state pays the local taxing jurisdiction the owner's property tax, and then collects accumulated principal and interest when the home is vacated by the owner or when the owner chooses to pay off the loan before that time.[130] Well over 10,000 such loans have been written. With appropriate targeting, this approach could be used by the state to relieve housing costs

TABLE 31

POTENTIAL REDUCTION IN EXCESSIVE HOUSING EXPENSE BURDENS AFTER RECEIPT OF REVERSE MORTGAGE PAYMENTS

	Percentage who spend more than 40% of their incomes on regular housing costs*	Percentage who need to spend more than 40% after reverse mortgage payment	Percentage reduction in excessive housing expense burden rate
Singles and Couples	12%	6%	50%
Singles	17	7	59
aged 75 and more	18	5	72
low income**	46	18	57
low income, aged 75 or more	29	8	72
Couples	6	4	33
head aged 75 or more	5	2	60
low income	41	24	41
low income, head aged 75 or more	16	7	56

*Housing costs include property taxes, utilities, fuel, garbage collection and, when any debt remains, mortgage payments.
**Income less than 150 percent of the poverty line.
SOURCE: Tabulated from the 1983 Annual Housing Survey
Bruce Jacobs, "The National Potential of Home Equity Conversion"

without relying extensively on the public fisc. Another approach some states and localities have chosen is to issue deferred payment loans for home repair. Such loans are typically income-conditioned.

In addition to affordability, another threat to independent living for senior citizens is the potential need for human assistance in daily functioning. As discussed earlier, those who are single or old-old face higher risk of need for such care. However, this demographic profile also is associated with higher potential reverse mortgage payments. In fact, home equity conversion is a promising private financing option for either direct payment for services at home or payment for long-term care insurance.[131] Here again, the demographic profile of risk is the same as the profile of opportunity to get most out of one's home equity.

How much impact could reverse mortgages have in New York State? On the one hand, the promise of this concept is limited by the lower rate of home ownership compared with the rest of the nation. Yet property values in some areas of the state are quite a bit higher than the national average. This is especially true downstate, which also has the most substantial affordability problems. Reliable estimates of the potential of home equity conversion in New York will require further analysis of census data.

Several words of caution are in order here. The decision to convert home equity into income is a serious one, in both financial and emotional terms. Home equity represents the bulk of most borrowers' assets, and spending some for housing expenses or health care means not having it to spend in other ways. Also, bequests must necessarily decline in size. The Depression generation is generally reluctant to take on any debt, even if it does not require monthly servicing.

Quite often, those who might need more income are widows who come from a generation in which women did not routinely make major financial decisions. They may be pressured by short-run problems that could be better addressed in other ways. More generally, the economic, familial, and housing situations of potential borrowers should all be considered before any equity is converted. There are various risks associated with different kinds of reverse mortgage plans for both borrower and lender. Fortunately, many of these risks have been analyzed by a number of individuals and organizations. The American Association of Retired Persons now has a center set up to provide relevant information about home equity conversion, with a special focus on consumer protection. Adequate counseling is a must for any home equity conversion program to serve elderly participants effectively.

Another concern about this kind of financial instrument has been its implications for public assistance program eligibility and benefit levels. Some have expressed the fear that Supplemental Security Income or Medicaid benefits would be withdrawn if older participants began to use this currently exempt asset. While the Social Security Administration has indicated that proceeds from reverse mortgages are loan disbursements and not income to be counted for Supplemental Security Income benefit determination, no such ruling has been made for Medicaid. To the extent that Medicaid expenses for the state could be reduced if reverse mortgages were used to finance long-term care insurance, there is a potential benefit for New York as well as for elderly homeowners. The state should consider various ways in which these gains might be made attractive to both parties.

Other states have been active in setting up reverse mortgage programs. In Connecticut, for example, low-income elderly homeowners can now take out loans from the state housing finance agency without having to repay them until they die or leave their homes. Both Maryland and Virginia have developed home equity lines of credit for senior citizens who could spend their equity when necessary without committing themselves to a specific monthly loan amount.

Demand for home equity conversion has been quite modest in this infancy of its development. There have been just over 3500 older homeowners who have spent some of their equity while remaining in their homes (excluding the much greater number who have deferred their property taxes).[132] Even when the various risks have been internalized and potential consumer and supplier knowledge is more complete, it is unlikely that anything like a majority of the elderly with home equity will choose such an option. (Recall national surveys suggesting that most elderly people say they are not financially strapped.) Yet, for most older homeowners, home equity is and will be the major untapped private resource available for housing expenses, health care, or other purposes.

Older New Yorkers in the Year 2000

It is by now a well-known truism that we are an aging society. New York State is no exception to this rule. While it is impossible to forecast with complete precision, there is sufficient information to make some firm predictions regarding the state's elderly population at the turn of the century. Specifically:

The number of New Yorkers aged 65 and older will substantially increase in both absolute and relative terms, making up a larger percentage of the population than in 1980.

While the young-old will become somewhat more numerous, the old-old population will increase dramatically.

Absent unexpected changes in morbidity and mortality rates and living arrangements, there will be substantial pressures on both informal and formal care systems in New York.

Interest will increase in housing options that combine housing with health care and social services.

The "graying" of the suburbs will redistribute New York's elderly population, with as yet unclear implications for government services and financing.

In 1985, New York State released its official population projections through the year 2010.[133] The population aged 65 or older is predicted to rise from 2,160,767 in 1980 to 2,700,742 in 2000, a 25 percent increase. The elderly's share of New York's population will rise from 12.3 percent to 14.5 percent. Looked at another way, about 540,000 older New Yorkers will account for 55 percent of the net total state population increase during this twenty-year period!

These figures must be viewed with some caution (as most forecasts should). They are based on assumptions about in-migration and out-migration rates (for both elderly and nonelderly groups) and age-specific mortality and fertility rates. Since each of these rates has varied somewhat over time, demographers must rely partially on some prudent "guess-timates" in their projection methodology. While substantial changes (for example in mortality rates of the elderly) are possible over the next decade, it is inconceivable that the dramatic increase of New York's older population will fail to materialize.

Perhaps more important than the rise in the numbers of senior citizens will be the changing balance between the old-old and the young-old. The population moving into their late sixties in 2000 are the children of the Depression. This generation is smaller than it might have been if their parents faced better economic conditions. The result is that there will be little change in the young-old population. The 70-74 age group will increase by 15 percent, while the 65-69 group will actually shrink by about two percent. Expansion in the higher age ranges rises from 37 percent in the 75-79 group to a startling 108 percent for those 85 and older. In total, the old-old (aged 75 or older) are projected to increase from two-fifths of New York's elderly population to one-half.

Table 32 documents the pattern of age change from 1980 to 2000 in each of the state's regions. Throughout the state, the old-old show higher rates of population increase, though there are substantial variations across regions. Especially noteworthy is the contrast between New York City, which has the largest decline in the young-old population and the smallest increase of the old-old, and Long Island, which has the largest increase of population in all age groups. These differences reflect the impact of the post-war housing boom and the rapid expansion of suburban communities after Levittown paved the way for this new housing pattern. As these pioneers have aged in place, the "graying of suburbia" has emerged as an important trend.

What makes the changing age distribution so critical is that the old-old population has heretofore been beset by lower incomes, higher rates of spouselessness, and greater risk of need for human assistance in daily functioning. The combined impact of these three factors has led to a much lower rate of independent living in the community and higher risk of living in a nursing home, mental hospital, or other group quarters.

There is some hope that rates of institutionalization may decrease in the next decade or so. Each new cohort entering old age appears to be somewhat better off financially than previous cohorts. If this pattern continues, elderly people will be better able to afford formal services or home remodeling that might extend their stay in the community.

TABLE 32

PROJECTED PERCENTAGE CHANGES IN THE ELDERLY POPULATION 1980-2000

REGION	65-69	70-74	75-79	80-84	85+	All 65+
			AGE GROUP			
BUFFALO	(11%)*	24%	54%	64%	107%	30%
ROCHESTER	1	24	47	50	83	30
SYRACUSE	(3)	25	61	60	96	33
SOUTHERN TIER	(3)	15	41	45	79	24
UPPER HUDSON	(9)	10	35	44	93	20
NORTH COUNTRY	6	18	44	50	87	30
MID HUDSON	15	21	38	36	68	28
NEW YORK CITY	(12)	(2)	14	24	123	11
NORTHERN NYC SUBURBS	6	21	39	42	111	30
LONG ISLAND	25	66	46	86	124	65
NEW YORK STATE	(2%)	15%	37%	43%	108%	25%

SOURCE: Calculated from *Official Population Projections from New York State Counties, 1980-2010.*

Decreasing mortality rates for men may result in less widowhood for women in advanced age groups. If medical science can make substantial inroads in reducing morbidity rates for those diseases that generate needs for other humans' help, independent living will be extended.

There are also reasons for concern, however, about a possible increase of institutionalization rates. Reduction in mortality rates for heart attack or cancer may allow more people to fall victim to paralyzing strokes or Alzheimer's disease, thus increasing dependence. Also, divorce rates have increased sharply from the levels faced in prior decades. While 4.5 percent of New Yorkers aged 65 or older in 1980 were either divorced or separated from their spouses, 10.3 percent of the 45 to 64 age group were in this situation.[134] If those people fail to remarry or team up with others in households, the primary source of informal care will be missing. The second most frequent source of informal care has previously been the services donated by older persons' children, in the great majority of cases their daughters. Today, however, full-time work is the rule rather than the exception for middle-aged women. The next cohorts entering advanced middle age (i.e., the baby boomers) have even higher labor force participation rates. The future does not look all that promising for familial-based informal care. (Yet, the great bulk of care is still supplied by family and friends, and one should not underestimate the degree to which families will struggle to provide such care.)

While it is very risky to estimate rates of institutionalization at the turn of the century, a crude projection for this purpose provides much food for thought. Age-group-specific rates of institutionalization were first calculated for each of the regions in the state using the 1980 PUMS data. These rates were then applied to the official population projections to calculate total numbers who would not be living in residential housing in the year 2000. Table 33 lists the estimated percentage changes in the numbers of institutionalized persons in each age group in each region. The projected figures are substantially higher for certain regions, particularly

TABLE 33

PROJECTED PERCENTAGE INCREASES IN THE ELDERLY INSTITUTIONAL POPULATION, 1980-2000

REGION	65-69	70-74	75-79	80-84	85+	All 65+
BUFFALO	(17%)*	29%	63%	74%	100%	69%
ROCHESTER	2	34	34	47	83	57
SYRACUSE	4	25	54	48	68	54
SOUTHERN TIER	5	28	43	62	108	69
UPPER HUDSON	(10)	16	25	51	63	44
NORTH COUNTRY	5	12	45	54	59	47
MID HUDSON	26	67	49	39	50	35
NEW YORK CITY	(8)	(3)	8	30	126	54
NORTHERN NYC SUBURBS	10	39	42	49	83	56
LONG ISLAND	31	69	90	91	118	91
NEW YORK STATE	6%	23%	39%	52%	99%	60%

*Numbers in parentheses are percentage decreases.
SOURCE: Institutionalization rates calculated from 1980 PUMS data. Population changes calculated from *Official Population Projections for New York State Counties 1980-2010*.

Long Island, and certain age groups, particularly those over age 85. While these figures are necessarily crude, given the simplistic methodology employed, the results are dramatic enough to suggest the magnitude of the prospective threat to independent living among older New Yorkers.

The central theme that emerges from these results is that there may be a need for substantial increases in institutional facilities for the elderly throughout New York State. The combined impact of high rates of institutionalization and large increases in the old-old population will exert strong pressure on care-giving systems. In fact, over 80 percent of the projected growth in nursing home, mental hospital, and other group quarter populations is accounted for by the increase in persons aged 80 or older.

The projected overall expansion of institutional beds is just over 79,000 (from 132,000 to 211,000). An especially dramatic change could occur in Long Island, where a rise of nearly 18,000 beds would nearly double 1980 capacity. While it is not possible to estimate the changes in other suburban areas (since official state population projections do not differentiate between central city and suburban portions of counties), the graying of suburbia will surely bring strong pressures on the formal care systems in these communities.

There is relatively little certainty that institutionalization rates will be of this magnitude at the turn of the century. Several forces may combine to lower the rates at which older people must leave their apartments and homes to enter nursing homes or mental hospitals. Perhaps the most substantial inhibiting factor is simply that very few people want to go into institutions if they can possibly avoid it. Beyond the emotional trauma often surrounding this housing change is the high expense of institutional stays that may stretch out months or years. At annual rates of more than $30,000, extended residence in a nursing home will eat up the assets of most New Yorkers quickly. The incentive to avoid institutionalization should increase the demand for housing alternatives outside of nursing homes.

In recent years there have been several initiatives (mostly proposed, a few tried) directed at allowing older people to remain at home instead of having to move out because of physical (and associated financial) inadequacies. As discussed in the next section, these housing alternatives will receive more attention (and perhaps more support) as the demographic pressure builds. Major medical breakthroughs might dramatically extend healthy life and contract physical dependence in old age, but it would be foolhardy to base future policies on this expectation.

Given the uncertainties in predicting independent living, efforts to project the older population's use of New York's housing stock in the year

2000 must be rather tentative. New York State last released official household projections just over a decade ago, without benefit of the 1980 Census results.[135] While a thorough analysis of changes in the elderly headed housing stock is beyond the scope of this research, it is useful to make a few very rough calculations to get some feel for the magnitude of increases that may occur.

The methodology employed for this purpose is similar to the one used for projecting rates of institutionalization. For each age grouping in each of the ten state regions, 1980 household headship rates were calculated. These headship rates were then applied to projected age group population levels to estimate the total numbers of elderly households in the year 2000. Table 34 details the results.

The most noteworthy findings of this crude projection are the very slow growth in New York City and the remarkable growth on Long Island (as expected with the graying of the suburbs). The slightly lower increase in total elderly households in the state, compared with the projected percentage increase in population, is primarily a function of the lower household-headship rates of the old-old.

It is a bit difficult to estimate reliably the tenure breakdown of elderly headed units in the year 2000. Unless circumstances change dramatically, however, it is quite clear that a higher percentage of New York's senior citizens will own their homes. Recall that New York City, which drastically reduces the statewide home ownership rate, will have the slowest growth. As well, aging suburbs are dominated by high owner occupancy rates.

Some hint of the tenure changes to come are found in the housing characteristics of the 45- to 64-year-old age cohort living in New York State in 1980.[136] In 1980, one-quarter of all aged households were suburban owners, while the figure for the younger cohort was three-eighths. Overall the home ownership rate of those 45 to 64 was 61 percent.

Not only do those in this age group own more homes, they own bigger and better homes. On average, homes owned by those 45 to 64 in 1980 had more rooms (6.4 vs. 5.8) than did the homes currently occupied by older owners. They were also less likely to be substandard as measured in this study (seven percent vs. eight percent). Finally, the estimated average value of the younger cohorts' homes was 22 percent higher than for current elderly homeowners. (All this bodes well for the future of home equity conversion.)

A variety of developments in the housing markets of New York (and elsewhere) could possibly change the plans of many thousands of the state's next cohorts of aged residents. Economic growth may be faster (or slower) than expected, inevitably having an impact on the capacity of both

TABLE 34

PROJECTED INCREASE IN ELDERLY HOUSEHOLDS, 1980-2000

REGION	Number of households in 1980	Projected households in 2000	Percent increase
BUFFALO	98,100	124,604	27%
ROCHESTER	66,100	85,343	29
SYRACUSE	81,200	106,399	31
SOUTHERN TIER	86,800	115,853	33
UPPER HUDSON	75,000	88,138	18
NORTH COUNTRY	44,400	55,210	24
MID HUDSON	52,600	67,019	27
NEW YORK CITY	617,000	680,234	10
NORTHERN NYC SUBURBS	78,900	106,091	34
LONG ISLAND	132,300	216,660	64
NEW YORK STATE	1,332,400	1,645,461	23%

SOURCE: Calculated from New York State sample, 1980 PUMS data and *Official Population Projections for New York State Counties, 1980-2010*

old and young to afford various housing options. The aging of the population may put sufficient financial pressures on all levels of government to reconsider the ways in which income and property of the elderly are taxed, thereby changing the effective price of housing (or of remaining in this state) as well as disposable income. For some families, it may no longer be financially possible to have each generation live independently. Public sector programs may liberate families from handling physical and fiscal dependence on a family-by-family basis. (Of course, this would imply tax burdens much higher than now anticipated.)

Another, perhaps more likely, possibility is that the increasing wealth of successive age cohorts will make affordability of a variety of alternative housing options more realistic than has heretofore been the case. To the extent that this is true, there may be much more migration (and housing mobility within communities) than in the past.

Housing choices might be dramatically affected by entirely plausible, if not expected, changes in the economy, in medical science, in family values, and in preferences, among other factors. Thus these rough estimates of aged populations, households, and institutionalization in the year 2000 provide some context for policy makers, rather than precise measures of housing and health circumstances.

Housing Options for the Aged in the Decades to Come

In recent years researchers, developers, social service practitioners, and advocates have proposed a wide variety of housing alternatives for the elderly. A few of these have actually been made available in the marketplace and have attracted many older residents (e.g., retirement communities). Others are being developed on a trial basis as both private and public funding has been made available (e.g., congregate housing). Still others are simply versions of housing options available for decades (e.g., "granny flats"). Most, however, are either still on paper or barely off the drafting board. It is impossible to know now which among these options, or others, will make the most sense to tomorrow's elderly population. There is going to be an inevitable sorting out process, with some initiatives succeeding and others bound for obscurity.

A helpful way to think about developing alternative housing options for the elderly is to divide them into those that help the elderly stay at home, if they wish, and those involving moves to other housing situations. It is also useful to distinguish public from private sector efforts in this development.

Aging in Place

If past behavior is a good predictor of future preferences, then most older people will want to remain where they have lived for such a long time. There are a variety of strategies that can be pursued by the elderly themselves and by the private sector to facilitate the continuation of independent living as household heads.

The capacity to pay for housing expenses is quite likely to vary substantially among different groups of New York's elderly in the decades to follow. The next cohorts of elderly household heads will have higher incomes and more assets as they enter old age than did their predecessors. Also, as discussed previously, there will be more homeowners among them, and their homes will be more valuable. However, the greatest percentage increase in elderly household heads will be among those aged 75 or older, a group characterized by much increased risk of financial and physical threats to independent living.

For the old-old whose income leaves them financially strapped, home equity will remain the largest untapped financial resource that could be used to pay for housing costs (or medical or other related service expenses). Reverse mortgages and other forms of home equity conversion will be especially helpful to low-income widows (and widowers) whose shorter life expectancy could allow for substantial income supplementation without the threat of outliving these assets (see Table 30).

Another strategy that could be pursued by low-income elderly homeowners is to set up separate housing units in unused portions of their homes. These "accessory apartments" provide a supplemental income stream and have, in fact, been utilized by a small (albeit as yet uncounted) number of older owners. In some cases, tenants pay a portion of their rent on an in-kind basis by doing minor repair or maintenance work or other household chores. A problem with this private housing alternative, however, has been local zoning laws that prohibit the conversion of single family homes into multidwelling units. Whether local communities will have a change of heart on this issue is uncertain.

A private option available to both owners and renters is shared housing. By having others move in, aged heads are relieved from some housing expenses and household duties, thus extending the period in which they can age in place. Though such living arrangements have become socially accepted (witness the "Golden Girls" television series), and several home-sharing programs have been set up to help match older people with new housing partners, there has not yet been a large-scale demand for this housing alternative. A perceived loss of privacy seems to be the major barrier encountered by programs promoting shared housing. How future aged heads will weigh this against the benefits of financial and other assistance remains to be seen.

Physical infirmities present perhaps the greatest threat to remaining in one's home. Absent unexpected changes in morbidity rates, the burgeoning old-old population will have to cope with these limitations if they are to live independently. One approach to encourage successful functioning in housing units is to modify them so the elderly can more easily cope with bathrooms, staircases, and the like. A good deal of knowledge about how such modifications can be made has been accumulated, but consumer willingness to pay for them has not yet been substantial, and some homes are simply not amenable to such changes at reasonable prices.

In recent years, the private market for at-home services for the disabled elderly has grown substantially. Such help may vary in intensity from minor chores to bathing and dressing those dependent on such assistance. In the future, increasing real incomes will almost surely combine with the decreasing availability of informal care givers to accelerate this expansion.

Home care would be much more affordable if the risk of need for these services was pooled in the form of private insurance plans. Some companies have already included home-care provisions in long-term care insurance they offer, and more are likely to do so. However, insurers have been understandably wary in pricing such plans. This is because they are fearful that those disproportionately likely to need care will buy the insurance (adverse selection), and that insurance-paid home care will inevitably substitute for some amount of informal care otherwise provided by family members (moral hazard).

Other forms of risk-sharing to pay for at-home services are currently under development. A "social health maintenance organization" (SHMO) provides a variety of services in addition to traditional medical care on an as-needed basis to aged participants who have subscribed to the program. Several demonstrations of this concept are currently underway, but whether the plans are cost-effective at a price acceptable to potential consumers is not yet known.[137] A related concept, "life care in the community," would graft the insurance/service components of life care communities (discussed below) in a policy that could be purchased by the elderly who would like to live in their homes as long as possible, rather than pay the substantial initial endowment and monthly costs of a life care community.

The public sector has a major role to play in assisting the aged to remain in their homes. Chief among these is the continuation of the various subsidies (both direct payment and tax relief) now given to the older population as they stay in their housing units. There are, however, major constraints that limit the impact of these programs. Not all older people who are eligible for direct subsidy (rental assistance, home repair grants, and so forth) can be served under current levels of funding. The great expansion in the older population (especially among the old-old, who are likely to have low incomes) will put further pressure on federal (and, in some cases, state and local) budgets.

New York probably can have more leverage in the support of private options that facilitate aging in place. Regulatory changes (e.g., allowing long-term reverse mortgages to be offered in the state) could open up additional privately financed alternatives. Local zoning changes (e.g., permitting accessary apartments) also might be appropriate. The state could serve as a center for information exchange, consumer (and producer) protection, and coordination, where possible, between public and private developers of housing alternatives. The focus here should not be on centralized decision making. Rather, it should help bring efficiencies into the development process.

It would seem sensible for New York State to follow the lead of others in establishing a property tax deferral program. If housing affordability is as serious a problem as the analysis in this study suggests, then a home equity loan program to pay property taxes might help many older homeowners. There need not be extensive state subsidization— interest rates could be set to cover program costs. However, there might be some income-targeted subsidy in such a program. Its cost would certainly be much less than the property tax exemption currently offered in the state.

The population projections discussed earlier pointed to an important trend in the location of the elderly's homes. New York State should pay explicit attention to the implications of the aging of the suburbs. Social services, publicly financed long-term care, property tax bases, and other governmental activities at the local level can be expected to change, dramatically in some cases. If the elderly are to remain in their homes in suburban communities, new governmental initiatives may be in order. These problems should be thought about now.

Moving to Other Housing

Though several hundred thousand aged people in the nation have moved to retirement communities in the sunbelt and elsewhere, most moves by the elderly are, in fact, made within the same community (or state).[138] A variety of private sector alternatives have been chosen by older people not wanting to (or not being able to) move a great distance. Most of these moves have simply been from one housing unit to another available in the general marketplace. However, a variety of other options have been (or may be) offered to the aged.

For many of those who have income or physical limitations, moving to a shared housing situation can be a viable alternative. There has been a good deal of recent interest in group homes in this regard. However, there are even more barriers to be faced by those choosing this alternative than by those accepting other residents into their homes. For example, the mover is faced with the loss of the comfort of functioning in a familiar setting and with the loss of complete control over her environment. Yet, for many who feel they must move, such a new group home environment may be far preferable to other affordable housing alternatives.

Another option, which does preserve control over one's home, is the "granny flat." This rather quaint term refers to a housing unit (usually temporary, like a mobile home) on the property of a relative, typically a child. The approach preserves some privacy for both parties. Here again, zoning restrictions have stood in the way of this housing alternative.

Physical infirmities may force elderly residents to move. However, there are a wide variety of circumstances in which such moves take place. Some may be planned before the onset of disabling conditions. One that pools the risk of disability is the life care (or continuing care) retirement community, which combines housing with social and health services available on a for-pay or insurance basis. Entry into one of these units is a serious decision, for it typically commits a significant fraction of the assets of those who make this choice. There are a substantial number of these throughout the nation,[139] but they are not available in New York State.[140] Some of these plans have gone bankrupt (mostly because of inadequate financial planning or insurance plan development). However, now there is much more research available to focus on how to deal with these problems, and in recent years the demand for this housing option has increased without the previous management difficulties.[141]

While we have projected a very substantial rise in the number of older New Yorkers who will live in nursing homes, institutionalization will undoubtedly remain perceived as perhaps the least desirable alternative. A multiplicity of housing arrangements in the community have offered a mixture of services to allow the disabled to remain outside of nursing homes. Many of these are classified as "residential care homes." This term actually has been used for housing setups of varied types. Depending on which services and personnel are available, they have been called "domiciliary care," "adult foster homes," or "congregate care homes."[142] Essentially halfway houses between normal community dwelling units and nursing institutions, these living options will probably continue to play an important role as alternative housing. Little is known about the cost-effectiveness of the various plans. Yet it seems inevitable that workable, affordable housing options of these types will evolve as a growing number of disabled people who feel they must leave their homes seek to avoid being institutionalized.

Elderly people also receive public sector help if they choose to move to other housing. Those over age 55, for example, receive a $125,000 exemption from capital gains taxation when they sell their homes. At the other end of the income spectrum, the elderly garner a disproportionate share of publicly subsidized housing units.[143]

Undoubtedly, the availability of public sector financing of nursing home stays (though financially painful to qualify for) will continue through Medicaid and, quite possibly, a governmentally run catastrophic long-term-care insurance plan. The most problematic aspect to public sector financing is that, if it becomes more easily available, rates of institutionalization will almost certainly increase, because public monies will to some degree replace private funds and informal care. If the federal and state governments extensively finance living in settings like congregate housing, their budgets will be similarly affected.

State and local government can facilitate options for moving through regulatory changes (e.g., allowing continuing care retirement communities and granny flats). Also, as with options to stay at home, the state should act as an information source and, where productive, a coordinating body.

Inevitably, many more public and private sector activities in the area of housing the elderly will be thought of (and some will actually be tried). At this stage, we are long on suggestions and short on knowledge and experience.[144] The economic efficiency (or inefficiency) of most of these options remains unknown. The marketability of various approaches (both in the private and the public sector) is yet to be tested. Predicting what will work and what will not is at least difficult and probably a fool's errand.

However, some general assertions are in order. The private sector will continue to provide the great bulk of housing options chosen by the elderly. And the elderly will do the choosing. The housing needs of the aged will be defined by their preferences, capabilities, and resources. Government should, however, continue to play an important role in facilitating the development of options.

Finally, though perhaps foolishly, we make one prediction. Housing options that internalize the risk of long-term care costs will find a growing demand as the population of old-old New Yorkers dramatically increases.

9

Conclusions

New York State finds itself at a crossroads. A growing state economy has propelled more people into suitable housing than ever before. Many of those New Yorkers fortunate enough to own housing have found their properties to have appreciated to levels previously unimagined. For these households, increasing home values assure there will be little cause for financial worry in the future.

At the same time, an increasing number of New Yorkers have found themselves on the sidelines of these developments. The more fortunate struggle to save enough to keep pace with the increasing downpayments that rapidly rising housing prices require, wondering whether they will ever be homeowners. The less fortunate confront much more painful choices over whether limited financial resources should go to shelter, clothing, or food.

There is little doubt that the crucial housing policy issue facing New York State today is the shortage of affordable housing. State and local governments have responded to the critical shortage of affordable housing by developing programs and devoting resources to housing at levels far higher than ever before. In part, this response has been dictated by the withdrawal of the federal government from its role as the primary public provider of housing services. But, despite the increased commitment of resources, state and local governmental responses have proven to be inadequate for stemming the burgeoning problem.

The inability to solve the affordable housing problem stems from a confluence of forces. First, one should place the affordability problem in budgetary context. The sheer magnitude of the affordable housing problem greatly exceeds the level of commitment state and local governments historically have been willing to devote to housing services. The cost gap between household income and the rental cost of affordable housing was estimated to exceed $1.8 billion annually (1980 dollars). Even doubling state and local governmental housing expenditures will leave many deserving households with high housing cost burdens.

Growth in the state's population and changes in household composition will make demands on housing services that will put additional pressure on governments' ability to respond to the affordable housing crisis. Projected population growth and household formation rates will require sizable additions to the stock of adequate housing by the year 2000. Unless the availability of public subsidies is expanded or steps are taken to reduce the cost of producing new housing, many households will enter the next century with excessive housing cost burdens.

The supply of affordable, adequate housing for low- and moderate-income New Yorkers will be further constrained by the aging of the housing stock. In the central cities of New York State, over 50 percent of the housing stock was built before 1939. Housing is a long-lived asset if maintained, but much of this older housing has been occupied by tenants with low rent-paying capacity. Without sufficient maintenance, even the most solidly built housing will decline. By the year 2000, over 70 percent of the state's housing stock will be more than 40 years old.

Further upward pressure on housing prices is also likely as land in the New York City metropolitan area becomes increasingly scarce. Land is essentially in fixed supply, so the increasing scarcity of land in the New York City metropolitan area assures that any new housing that is affordable to low- and moderate-income tenants must be heavily subsidized.

Scarce land is partly the result of development patterns shaped by local land-use decisions. As long as barriers to more intensive residential development remain, housing prices will necessarily reflect high land costs. The well-publicized problems of young adults being unable to afford living in the communities where they grew up, or of housing prices outstripping service workers' ability to afford housing, will be exacerbated.

Not long ago, such a gloomy prognosis would be tempered by the addition of new, federally subsidized housing, affordable for low- and moderate-income households. But, since the federal government has essentially withdrawn from new production programs, this is no longer the case. Even worse, not only are there fewer new units entering the low- and moderate-income stock, but the number of existing subsidized units may actually decline. Portions of both the federally subsidized housing stock and the state's subsidized Mitchell-Lama housing projects may soon be removed from governmental control.[145] When existing contracts which limit allowable rent levels expire, we can expect building owners to opt out of public subsidy arrangements and replace low- and moderate-income tenants with residents able to pay market rents. We have just begun to see the beginning of this process. It is too early to tell how serious a threat this represents to the state's subsidized stock.

These considerations suggest the task ahead is formidable. But recognizing and identifying the problems ahead is the first important step in developing a policy agenda. Understanding what New York State can do, and how it can most effectively pursue its goals, will provide an important foundation for developing housing policies for the next century.

This study examined a number of policy options that state policy makers can pursue. Policy makers should develop their policy responses cognizant of the task before them and of the uncertainties ahead. Foremost is the recognition that future policy options will be constrained by the state's limited resources. The extent of the affordable housing problem is far too large for the state to solve on its own.

Even a mass infusion of resources will not be sufficient to solve all housing problems. The results of housing policy interventions are often unpredictable. Their outcomes depend on the behavioral responses of individuals, the structure of the housing market, the activities of the federal government, and the willingness of local units to cooperate. Policies designed without recognition of these complex inter-relationships are likely to have numerous unintended consequences.

Some straightforward guidelines can be proposed, however, for thinking about how these policy options should be considered.

The State should continue to recognize its role as an intermediary in the area of housing policy. Coordination and integration become increasingly important as the numbers of actors increase. There will always be gaps in federal policy and a need for coordination across local jurisdictional boundaries. Explicit attention should be devoted to developing mechanisms for identifying these gaps and coordinating the activities of local units.

Recognizing its role as policy coordinator, the state should press both the federal government and local government to maintain their level of effort. Federal abdication from the lead role in housing policy leaves a vacuum that no smaller unit of government can fill. It is unrealistic to expect the state to fill the gap.

The state also has a role to play in encouraging local policies. New York State has ceded much of its authority to local governments. Attempts to lower the cost of producing housing through major changes in the regulatory structure of New York State cannot be accomplished without local cooperation. Recognizing that local governments may not share state housing goals, the state should look for ways of making these programs more palatable to local officials. New creative mechanisms are required to elicit local cooperation.

The state should recognize the role of nongovernmental actors and continue to help coordinate their activities. The active involvement of nongovernmental institutions in developing affordable housing creates an additional coordination challenge for the state. The affordable housing problem is simply too large and public resources too scarce to fail to make full use of the voluntary sector. Non-profit developers must often combine a number of programs to allow them to develop affordable housing. The state could serve a valuable role in easing the coordination pressures that meeting multiple deadlines and program regulations demand.

The state must develop a clearer understanding of the cost-effectiveness of various housing policies. The magnitude of the affordability problem, relative to the state's financial constraints, mandates that more systematic analysis of current and future housing strategies be conducted. Future policy decisions should be based on better answers to questions about the cost-effectiveness of program efforts. Key among these is a better understanding of the relative benefits of different programs for a specified budget size, an understanding of the distributional consequences of different housing strategies, and an examination of how policies can be altered and improved.

The state must be careful to maintain policy flexibility. If there are any certainties they are that the federal role will change, market conditions will alter, and investment opportunities will vary. It is difficult to foretell when locational shifts, policy changes, or attitude changes will occur. State programs should be created which are flexible enough to accommodate change. In part, this requires that the state actively monitor the success and outcomes of its policy experiments. Housing dollars are too scarce to get tied to strategies that have yet to be established as successful.

Notes

1. Nearly 80 percent of poor renter households paid more than 35 percent of their income on housing in 1985. The corresponding figure for homeowners was 65 percent. *See* Center on Budget and Policy Priorities (1989).

2. For a detailed discussion of the relative well-being of different generations *see* Levy (1988).

3. Governmental programs have also been developed for less laudable goals, serving as conduits for political payoffs and rewards. The recent investigation into improper activities at HUD aside, we focus on desirable housing goals.

4. *See* Congressional Budget Office (1988).

5. *See* Governor's Housing Task Force (1988).

6. *See* Palmer and Sawhill (1982).

7. A full accounting of state housing policy should also include other state activity such as regulatory impacts, land-use controls, rent regulations, and building and construction codes.

8. For instance, in 1987 SONYMA provided $700 million for below market rate mortgages for affordable housing. HFA has statutory authority to issue $3 billion in bonds to be used to provide low cost mortgages for multifamily housing.

9. This framework is derived from Anthony Downs' analysis of federal housing policy (1976).

10. Missing from this list is mention of the goal to balance regional political interests. Many policy initiatives are undertaken in New York State in a way that balances upstate and downstate constituencies. We prefer to think of these political considerations as constraints on the choice of policies rather than as an objective itself.

11. A more detailed description of these programs can be found in the Appendix.

12. The 1980 PUMS data was provided through the Inter-university Consortium of Political and Social Research (ICPSR). I would like to acknowledge their assistance in providing the data tapes.

13. This population projection is used by the New York State Project 2000

Population Report titled, "The People of New York: Population Dynamics of a Changing State." I refer to this study in my report as the *Project 2000 Population Study*. The projected number of households is based on estimates presented later in this study.

14. Some housing analysts attribute this to a natural reduction in historical ownerships rates, following the rapid increase in ownership rates induced by the inflation driven decisions of the 1970s. *See also* Joint Center for Housing Studies (1987).

15. *See* DiPasquale (1988).

16. I define the ten housing regions to consist of the following counties:

1. Buffalo (Niagara, Erie)
2. Rochester (Orleans, Genesee, Wyoming, Monroe, Wayne, Livingston, Ontario)
3. Syracuse (Seneca, Cayuga, Cortland, Oswego, Onondaga, Madison, Oneida, Herkimer, Otsego)
4. Southern Tier (Chautauqua, Cattaraugus, Allegany, Steuben, Yates, Schuyler, Chemung, Tompkins, Tioga, Broome, Chenango, Delaware, Sullivan)
5. Upper Hudson (Fulton, Montgomery, Schenectady, Saratoga, Rensselaer, Schoharie, Albany, Greene, Columbia)
6. North Country (Jefferson, Lewis, St. Lawrence, Franklin, Clinton, Essex, Hamilton, Warren, Washington)
7. Mid-Hudson (Ulster, Orange, Dutchess)
8. New York City (New York, Richmond, Kings, Queens, Bronx)
9. Northern NYC Suburbs (Putnam, Westchester, Rockland)
10. Long Island (Nassau, Suffolk)

17. For an excellent analysis of the changing conceptions of what constitutes inadequate housing, *see* Salins (1986).

18. Unfortunately, the Census Bureau does not provide a complete accounting of housing costs for all households. The Census Bureau does not collect housing cost data on mobile homes, units on ten or more acres, units connected to a commercial establishment, two or more units in a structure, or condominiums. This peculiarity of Census data greatly diminishes the information available on apartment owners in New York State. Since this form of ownership is most common in New York City, it particularly influences the New York City results. I have elected to report on housing characteristics whenever I have usable data. Thus, the quality characteristics are based on the full sample while the housing cost variable only reports on those units for which the Census Bureau provides data. (Figures 7-12 are based solely on households that report housing cost data.) This excludes, as noted above, most condominium owners in New York City. To

the extent that condominium owners face differential housing costs, the reported excessive cost estimates would have to be altered. The NYC owner cost estimates should be viewed with this important caveat in mind.

19. I use this more inclusive measure becuse of the relatively high cost of living in New York State, to show that housing affordability is not only a problem of the poor, and to develop an estimate of the cost of a housing policy directed toward moderate income New Yorkers. In 1980, the poverty line for a family of four was $8,414. In 1988 the poverty line increased to $12,092.

20. *See* U.S. Census of Housing (1980).

21. The Annual Housing Survey, now called the American Housing Survey, allows more detailed analysis of housing inadequacy because it contains information on the degree of dilapidation of the structure. However, the AHS does not permit state-by-state analysis.

22. These percentages implicitly control for larger black household size because the poverty index is linked to both household resources and the number of family members.

23. For a detailed analysis of the housing conditions of black households, *see* Oliver and Price (1988).

24. The National Housing Task Force (1988) chooses to focus on the question of availability of housing. Since they are concerned with the supply of housing that is affordable to low-income households, I treat this as a special case of the affordability issue.

25. The housing affordability index measures the ability of the median-income family to afford the median-priced home. It is calculated and available from the National Association of Realtors.

26. The housing cost burdens are broken out somewhat differently in the AHS tables so I use the 35 percent standard for renters (the closest to the standard I report).

27. One of the most impressive exceptions has been the ability of the Nehemiah Project to construct housing affordable to low- and moderate-income tenants with relatively modest subsidy. However, a shortage of appropriate sites appears to have slowed down the rate at which these units are being developed (*New York Times*, September 24, 1987).

28. We caution the reader that the housing price and income numbers used here are based on the latest available statewide tabulations—the 1980 Census. To the extent that increases in rent have outraced increases in income, these numbers should be used as lower bound estimates. At the national level, from 1978 to 1985, housing costs of the median renter household increased 16 percent in real terms.

Since 1985, income increases and rent increases have been comparable (Center on Budget and Policy Priorities, 1989).

29. The poverty line for large families exceeded $6,000 in 1980.

30. *See* Talmas (1986).

31. Calculations from the PUMS data set.

32. Whether $1.8 million would close the gap is not at all certain. For one, since some non-poor households choose to live in low cost units, there may be insufficient units renting at the median rent to house all recipients. Further, it is not clear how an infusion of income will impact the housing market—will more units be built or will housing prices go up? Finally, will the availability of housing subsidies lead some households to diminish their work effort?

33. Later in this paper I analyze mortgage subsidies and capital grants programs aimed at helping households achieve ownership status. For that analysis I restrict eligibility to those households who could assume the financial responsibility of ownership.

34. I assume a ten percent equity position with a 30-year loan at a ten percent mortgage rate.

35. President Roosevelt signed the Emergency Price Control Act on January 30, 1942. The rent control provisions of this law were implemented in New York in 1943.

36. For a critique of existing management practices, *see* "Bleak House: DHCR at the Crossroads," Joint Assembly Committees' Investigation of Rent Administration in New York State, June 1987. For a description of recent improvements in administrative operations, *see* "The Office of Rent Administration: A Management Analysis," Governor's Office of Management and Productivity, November 1987.

37. For a sampling of opinion, *see* Block and Olsen (1981).

38. *See* Stegman (1984).

39. *See* Stegman (1985).

40. Since the inception of rent control, New York City vacancy rates have been consistently lower than non-controlled cities. Further, vacancy rates for the decontrolled stock are higher than for the controlled stock within New York City.

41. For an examination of the distribution of the aggregate benefits from rent control, *see* Linneman (1987).

42. The data in this section comes from the 1984 New York City Housing and Vacancy Survey.

43. I would like to thank Sharon McGroder for her calculations which form the basis of this chapter.

44. This estimate is their mid-range population estimate, and I use it as my best guess of the actual year 2000 total.

45. Of course, if affordable housing is less available in the next two decades than it was in the prior three, the conditions that would permit the continued decline of household size would be quite different.

46. It has been the persistent inability to maintain this level of vacancies that has led New York State policy makers to enact a variety of tenant protection measures.

47. This estimate exceeds my statewide estimate of nine percent because it is based on a broader definition of housing inadequacy that can be derived from the Annual Housing Survey but not from the Census data.

48. Evidence from the Experimental Housing Allowance Program points clearly to households choosing to spend additional resources on a variety of items, and not just housing. This was true even for those households who had the opportunity to upgrade their residences from substandard conditions.

49. For a good overview of the relationship between demographics and housing, *see* Sternlieb and Hughes (1986).

50. This figure is derived by dividing the number of projected households in the year 2000, assuming family size of 2.3 members, by the number of households in 1980.

51. *See Project 2000 Population Study*, p. 99.

52. In 1988 the national poverty rate for all families was 10.4 percent. For female headed households the rate was 33.5 percent. The poverty rate for households without female heads was 5.9 percent. ("Money Income and Poverty Status of Families and Persons in the United States: 1988, U.S. Department of Commerce, Bureau of Census, Current Population Reports).

53. We note that many of the strategies we discuss as demand side strategies could also be viewed as supply-side strategies. The distinction is primarily one of whether the subsidy is being provided to the supplier of housing services or the households demanding those services. We treat the two categories in turn.

54. Evidence from the Experimental Housing Allowance Program reveals that when payments were not tied to housing standards, approximately two-thirds of the recipients lived in substandard housing.

55. Hanushek and Quigley's (1981) estimates of the income elasticity of demand for housing are all below 1.0.

56. These cost estimates assume full participation of qualified households. It is unlikely that full participation would be achieved particularly if quality standards are tied to receipt of the subsidy. Nevertheless, these calculations provide a benchmark for understanding program costs. *See* Bradbury and Downs (1981).

57. Note that these estimates exclude households choosing to pay more than 30 percent of their income on apartments that have rents above the community median. On the other hand, they identify some low-income households as potential recipients, even if they would voluntarily choose to live in relatively cheap apartments at rent rates below 30 percent of their income.

58. We examine the simplest form of housing subsidy program to place the affordability problem and the resources it will take to solve it in some perspective. Housing allowance programs can also be designed to guarantee that recipients consume a certain quality of housing or that landlords make required code repairs.

59. Unless otherwise stated, the cost and coverage estimates that follow are based on a subsidy program where the region's median valued rental unit is used as the standard.

60. There are approximately 1.1 million renters in New York State with incomes below 150 percent of the poverty line.

61. We offer this as an example of the size of the subsidy problem, not as a statement about the desirability of subsidizing one group rather than another.

62. *See*, for example, A.B. Schnare, *Externalities, Segregation, and Housing Prices* (1974). For a somewhat different view, *see* Raymond Struyk, "Should Government Encourage Homeownership?" (1977).

63. The National Association of Realtors' data indicate that the median sales price for a home in the Northeast was $109,000 in 1987. For households with the state's median income level of $29,000, a $98,000 mortgage is supportable at 40 percent of household income. The $11,000 downpayment can be saved over a 3-year period if 12 percent of household income is put aside in savings each year.

64. Under TEFRA single family mortgage revenue bonds will no longer enjoy tax exempt status. Without the tax exempt status, SONYMA will no longer be able to provide below market rate mortgages unless it devises some other subsidy source.

65. Many of the demand side strategies can also be thought of supply strategies if the subsidies are provided directly to developers. We discuss this strategy for multifamily housing developers as a supply-side strategy in the case of up-front capital grants, energy cost saving investments, and property tax reductions.

66. The existence of high utility costs in a region may not necessarily create a

hardship for low-income renters since energy cost increases need not always get passed on to consumers. In the long run, the impact of increasing energy prices may be borne by owners of housing.

67. For an excellent discussion of these issues, *see* Struyk (1981).

68. Renters are able to claim a portion of their rental payments as property tax related and therefore can also take advantage of the circuit breaker.

69. For a detailed analysis of the Michigan circuit breaker program, *see* Rubinfeld and Wolkoff (1983).

70. *See* Bradbury and Downs, (1981).

71. The market for capital is national resulting in relatively small variation in financing rates from region to region.

72. *See* Durning and Quigley (1985).

73. For an examination of the role of negotiation in land use disputes, *see* Wheeler (1988).

74. For one of the first cases establishing the right of communities to zone, *see* Euclid vs. Ambler Realty.

75. A secondary consequence of income sorting has been racial segregation. Although the degree of racial sorting exceeds what income differences alone would imply, there is little doubt that local zoning codes have contributed to both types of sorting. Census data from 1980 show that in New York State median household income in central cities was $13,600, only 80 percent of the total SMSA level of $16,900. Further, only six percent of suburban households are nonwhite while 36 percent of central city households are nonwhite.

76. Recognition of these effects has recently led New York City officials to revise the local zoning code to allow higher density construction. Undoubtedly, other cities face similar circumstances.

77. The *President's National Urban Policy Report, 1984* claims that as much as 25 percent of the unit cost of a home is due to regulation.

78. The courts have had limited success in assuring that housing be provided to low- and moderate-income households. Despite the courts ruling on the Mount Laurel case in New Jersey, the presence of subsidized housing in affluent New Jersey suburbs has changed little.

79. Assemblyman David F. Gantt has introduced legislation, co-sponsored by Assemblymen Grannis, Boyland, Young, Patton, and Lopez, to establish a Fair Housing Act. This legislation would create a Council on Affordable Housing, which would evaluate mandated "Fair Share" housing plans from each municipality

in the state. The bill "seeks to insure that the citizens of this state have access to affordable housing where there is need, throughout the state, and determines that every municipality, whether village, town or city, has a legal and moral obligation to provide their 'fair share' of low and moderate income housing for the greater regoinal need." (Language from memorandum in support of Assembly Bill 6774.)

80. Witness the problems of finding prison sites; *see* Project 2000 "Report on Corrections and Criminal Justice."

81. *See Report of the Mayor's Blue Ribbon Panel, 1986.*

82. There are over six million existing units in New York State, and the average net addition to the stock is approximately 30,000 units annually.

83. *See* Stegman (1984).

84. *See* Felstein and Stegman (1987).

85. For a detailed treatment of this argument, *see* Wolkoff (1990).

86. Unless otherwise indicated, all statistics in this study are based on analysis of the 1980 Census of Housing one percent public use microdata sample (PUMS).

87. Percentages in various living situations do not add up to 100 due to rounding.

88. These figures are based on before-tax cash incomes of those living in the community. Though the aged are more likely to have low incomes so measured, when tax liabilities and noncash benefits are taken into account, the elderly income distribution (nationally) is about the same as for those who are less than 65 years old. *See* Jacobs (forthcoming).

89. *See* Weissert (1985).

90. Dependence on personal care is a very strong predictor of institutionalization. *See* Weissert and Scanlon (1983).

91. *See* Stone (1987).

92. *See* Weissert (1985).

93. *See* Jacobs and Weissert (1987).

94. This measure is used instead of the official poverty definition because the cost of living in New York is higher, on average, than in the rest of the nation. The official poverty line for a single elderly person in 1988 was $5,674. For a couple it was $7,158.

95. Some of the materials in this section were first published in Jacobs (1985).

96. *See* National Council on Aging (1981), p. 10.

97. *See* Rabushka and Jacobs, (1980), ch. 6.

98. Measuring the presence of other possible housing inadequacies would obviously increase the absolute percentage of substandard housing. Unfortunately, the decennial census data do not provide the opportunity to do this. Any such measurement should, however, be directly linked to threats to the resident's health or safety (*see* Rabushka and Jacobs [1980], ch. 5). In any event, national data using more complete measures of inadequacy indicate that the elderly's housing stock has been improving and is not significantly less adequate than younger persons' housing (*see* Jacobs [1985]).

99. *See* National Council on Aging (1981), p. 7.

100. *See* Commonwealth Fund Commission (1986).

101. *See* Rabushka and Jacobs, (1980), ch. 6.

102. *See* Jacobs (1985), pp. 136, 140.

103. Other evidence in support of the lower priority given housing quality by elderly homeowners comes from the sample analyzed by Rabushka and Jacobs. They found that only three percent of the homeowners interviewed in seven localities throughout the nation said they had a serious need for repair and could not pay for it. Separate multivariate analyses of these data found that increasing income did not substantially result in more home repairs or better quality of the house's condition. *See* Struyk and Soldo (1980) and Rabushka and Jacobs (1980), Appendix C.

104. *See* Rabushka and Jacobs (1980), p. 61.

105. *See* Reschovsky (n.d.) and Newman and Reschovsky (1987).

106. M. Powell Lawton has recently written:

In any case, the high level of satisfaction cannot be written off as an artifact. Rather, a justified assumption is that at least some part of this satisfaction comes from both active attachment to the residence and the feeling that a change to a new residence might be more risky than the status quo ... The phenomenon of emotional attachment to place is not well conceptualized at present and certainly not adequately researched.

See Lawton (1986), p. 66.

107. *See Statistical Abstract of the United States: 1986*, table 16.

108. *See* Wiseman (1986), pp. 74.

109. Derived from *New York State Project 2000 Report on Population*, pp. 16-17 and 1980 Census data.

110. *See* Jacobs (forthcoming).

111. *See* Struyk and Soldo (1980), pp. 68-71.

112. The data for the U.S. are drawn from the 1980 Annual Housing Survey national sample. Home ownership cost data are for single family homes on less than ten acres without any commercial establishment or medical office on the premises. Mobile homes and trailers are excluded.

113. In 1980, elderly homeowner housing costs in New York State averaged $261 per month, while renters paid an average of $211.

114. This difference reflects, in part, the investment nature of home ownership, as well as the flow of housing services home ownership provides.

115. *See* Struyk and Turner (1982), p. 12.

116. In 1986, the Census Bureau estimated that 55 percent of such income went unreported. See U.S. Bureau of the Census (1987).

117. *See* U.S. Bureau of the Census (1986), pp. 12, 22.

118. Much of this material is derived from Jacobs (1986) and (1985).

119. *See* U.S. Bureau of the Census (1986).

120. This probably means that most middle- and upper-income elderly renters have much more wealth in other kinds of financial assets than is the case nationally. It is quite unlikely, however, that many low-income New York renters have substantially more in the way of non-home equity wealth. If they did, we would expect higher incomes than are reported.

121. *See* Friedman and Sjogren (1981), p. 28.

122. *See* Garnett and Guttentag (1982). HELP is no longer accepting new participants, in most part because of political haggling in Buffalo.

123. These loans might be renewed and extended if sufficient appreciation in the home's value occurs. However, there is no contractual obligation to renegotiate the terms of the loan.

124. *See* Garnett and Guttentag (1984) and Leban (1984).

125. *See* Scholen, et al. (1984).

126. At this writing, there is no short run prospect of passing the required legislation.

127. In addition to Jacobs (1986), *see* Jacobs (1980).

128. These results are from "The National Potential of Home Equity

Conversion." The reader should note that these estimates are based on the Irma Plan, which is not available in New York State.

129. This analysis excludes elderly homeowners with relatives other than spouses in their homes.

130. Usually, below market interest rates are charged, but this need not be the case.

131. In addition to Jacobs (1986), *see* Jacobs and Weissert (1987). A recent study concludes that home equity conversion, in conjunction with long-term care insurance, would maximize the private sector's capacity to fund long-term care in the decades to come. *See* Rivlin and Wiener (1988).

132. This figure ignores the myriad of private family arrangements that accomplish the same goal. In France, investor purchase of homes from elderly people who may remain in them while receiving payments is a more widespread practice. The arrangement is called "rente viager."

133. *See* New York State Data Center (1978).

134. These results are from the 1980 PUMS data.

135. *See* New York Economic Development Board (1978).

136. It is not possible simply to extrapolate these household's characteristics as the pattern of aged housing (of the young old) in 2000, since migration, intrastate moves, family structure changes and the like will vary these characteristics.

137. *See* Leutz, et al. (1988).

138. *See* Golant (1987).

139. *See* American Association of Retired Persons (1984).

140. *See* Long Term Care Policy Coordinating Council (1985). Legislation introduced in 1989 would legalize this housing option in New York State, but its passage is uncertain.

141. *See*, for example: Winklevoss and Powell (1984).

142. *See* Mor, et al. (1986).

143. *See* Jacobs (1985).

144. For a recent review of some of the related issues, *see* Institute of Medicine and National Research Council (1988).

145. Clay (1987) estimates that 900,000 units will be eligible for market rate rentals by 1995.

Appendix: State Housing Programs

Direct Housing Programs

Low-Income Public Housing

The state has financed construction of 143 public housing projects totaling over 66,000 apartments, housing over 280,000 primarily low-income people. These programs operate through local public housing authorities, are financed through general bond obligations, and are supported by an annual state subsidy of over $40 million. Project modernization has been paid for by the Public Housing Modernization Program, budgeted for $13 million in 1988-89, and the federal Home Energy Assistance Program budgeted for approximately $1 million in 1988-89.

Middle-Income Public Housing

The state has pioneered two major efforts providing access to rental housing for households that are too rich to qualify for public housing but too poor to compete effectively in the private market. The Limited Dividend Housing Program provides property tax incentives to builders supplying moderately priced housing. This program, enabled under the Limited Dividends Company law of 1926, has attracted modest developer interest. Only 10,000 or so apartments have been built in the 22 projects under this program.

In 1955, the state enacted the Limited Profit Housing Companies Act, better known as the Mitchell-Lama Law. This act enabled the state to provide private developers with low cost finance and tax incentives for moderate income apartments. Financing for these projects has come through the Urban Development Corporation, the New York State Housing Finance Agency, as well as direct state loans. To date, 269 projects have been built containing over 100,000 apartments.

This program has been very successful in bringing new units on-line. However, the Mitchell-Lama program has not been self-supporting, forcing New York State to provide additional operating subsidies. The state has allocated over $166 million for Mitchell-Lama project repairs since 1980. The state has also assumed part of the financial responsibility for these projects in response to tenant pressures.

Low-Income Housing Trust Fund

This trust fund was established in 1985 with an allocation of $25 million per year for the following five years. The Low Income Housing Trust Fund provides up to $40,000 per unit to local development corporations, non-profit agencies, municipal governments, etc., for subsidizing the cost of rehabilitation or conversion of structures for low-income housing. The highly successful Nehemiah projects have been funded by this program.

Housing Development Fund

This $10 million revolving loan fund provides interest-free start-up money to nonprofit sponsors of middle-income housing. Since 1985, 110 projects totalling 22,089 apartments have used the Housing Development Fund.

Rural Area Revitalization Program

This program provides funds for brick and mortar type projects that would not be feasible without additional funding. Approximately $2 million has been appropriated for each of the past three years. Projects have included low and moderate income housing projects as well as commercial development. Rural areas are defined as cities, towns, and villages having a population of less than 20,000.

Rural Rental Assistance Program

This program provides direct rental subsides for low-income elderly and family tenants residing in multi-family projects built under the Farmers Home Administration programs. Since its inception the state has appropriated over $20 million in rental subsidies.

Infrastructure Trust Fund (1988)

A variety of housing related programs are funded under this legislation. Programs include: Low Income Turnkey Program, North Country Development Authority, Special Needs Housing Demonstration Program, Permanent Housing for the Homeless Program, and Infrastructure Development Demonstration Program.

Homeless Housing Assistance Program

This program is designed to provide grants to develop shelter for the homeless. $20 million was appropriated for 1988-89.

Administrative Oversight

New York State is responsible for the administration of a number of federal programs concerned with the fiscal and physical health of the public housing stock, as well as the rent paying ability of tenants. These programs include: Section 236 mortgage interest subsidies, rental assistance program and rent supplements, Section 8 existing housing programs, and the flexible subsidy program for Section 236 developments.

The state also provides seed money and income support to a number of community-based organizations through the Neighborhood Preservation Companies Program and the Rural Preservation Companies Program. Funding for 1985/86 totalled over $17 million.

Planning and Technical Assistance

Neighborhood Preservation Companies Program

Established in 1977, this program provides funds to neighborhood not-for-profit organizations for administrative and planning expenses. These organizations provide a variety of housing services from rehabilitation to counseling. Over $12 million was appropriated in 1988-89.

Section 107 Technical Assistance Program

DHCR provides funds and assistance to localities to promote the effective use of federal Community Development Block Grant funds.

Financing Programs

Housing Finance Agency

HFA loans the proceeds from the sale of tax-exempt bonds for the construction or rehabilitation of multi-family rental housing projects. In exchange for below market rate mortgages, developers must make available 20 percent of the units constructed for households below 80 percent of the region's median income, at a maximum rent of 30 percent of income.

HFA also runs the Affordable Housing Corporation. AHC is funded at $25 million annually. This program promotes home ownership by persons of low and moderate income, by providing financial assistance for the acquisition, construction, rehabilitation and improvement of owner occupied housing.

The State of New York Mortgage Agency

SONYMA offers below market mortgages through the sale of tax-exempt revenue bonds. Beneficiaries of the program receive below market rate financing, need only make a five percent downpayment and receive fixed rate loans. Beneficiaries must be first-time homebuyers except in targeted distressed areas. Income limits are placed on borrowers and value limits on the prices of the homes they purchase.

New York State Urban Development Corporation

UDC has financed 113 housing developments, totaling over 33,000 units throughout the state, by providing low-cost financing made possible by its bonding authority. In recent years, UDC has shifted focus to commercial development. UDC has unique powers to override local building and zoning codes. UDC primary funds were derived from the sale of tax-exempt bonds to private investors. As a result of the financial crisis of the mid-1970s, UDC's powers were severely circumscribed.

Regulatory Authority

Rent Control and Rent Stabilization

Rent controls exist in 64 municipalities including New York City, Albany, Buffalo, and a number of smaller villages and towns in the counties of Albany, Erie, Nassau, Rensselaer, Schenectady, and Westchester. DHCR administers both rent control and rent stabilization in New York City. In 1986 DHCR budgeted over $20 million for the administration of the rent control system.

Housing and Building Codes

The State Housing and Building Code, established January 1, 1984, sets the minimum quality standard for buildings across the state (except New York City). Housing quality standards can be enhanced by local mandate. Local governments are responsible for enforcement of the code unless ceded to the state by default.

Environmental Control

The site development approval process includes a number of regulatory requirements implemented by the State Department of Environmental Conservation. Most important are the State Environmental Quality Review Law, which requires developers to submit an environmental assessment for all proposed development, and the State Pollution Discharge Elimination System, which protects water quality.

Land-Use Controls

Zoning is a local power granted by the state constitution.

Bibliography

Aaron, H., *Shelter and Subsidies*, Brookings Institution, Washington, D.C., 1972.

Allen, G., Fitts, J., and Glatt, E., "The Experimental Housing Allowance Program," in *Do Housing Allowances Work?*, eds., K. Bradbury and A. Downs, Brookings Institution, Washington, D.C., 1981.

American Association for Retired Persons, *National Continuing Care Directory*, Scott, Foresman and Company, 1984.

Block, W. and Olsen, E., ed., *Rent Control. Myths and Realities*, The Fraser Institute, 1981.

Center on Budget and Policy Priorities, *A Place to Call Home. The Crisis in Housing for the Poor*, Washington, D.C., 1989.

Clay, P., "At Risk of Loss: The Endangered Future of Low-Income Rental Housing Resources," Neighborhood Reinvestment Corporation, Washington, D.C., 1987.

Commonwealth Fund Commission on Elderly People Living Alone, *Problems Facing Elderly Americans Living Alone*, Louis Harris and Associates, 1986.

Congressional Budget Office, *Current Housing Problems and Possible Federal Responses*, December 1988.

DiPasquale, D., "First Time Homebuyers: Issues and Policy Options," MIT Center for Real Estate Development, 1988.

Downs, A., *The Revolution in Real Estate Finance*, Brookings Institution, Washington, D.C., 1985.

Durning, D. and Quigley, J., "On the Distributional Implications of Mortgage Revenue Bonds and Creative Finance," *National Tax Journal*, Vol. XXXVIII, No. 4, December 1985.

Ellickson, R., "The Irony of "Inclusionary" Zoning," in *Resolving the Housing Crisis*, M. Bruce Johnson, ed., Ballinger Publishing Co., May 1987.

Felstein, C. and Stegman, M. "Towards the 21st Century: Housing in New York City," Commission on the Year 2000, May 1987.

Follain, J., ed., *Tax Reform and Real Estate*, Urban Institute, Washington, D.C., 1986.

Friedman, J. and Sjogren, J., "Assets of the Elderly as They Retire," *Social Security Bulletin* 44, No. 1, January 1981.

Friedman, J. and Weinberg, D., *The Economics of Housing Vouchers*, Academic Press, 1982.

Garnett, R. and Guttentag, J., "HELP in Buffalo," *Housing Finance Review* 1, 1982.

———. "The Reverse-Shared-Appreciation-Mortgage," *Housing Finance Review* 3, 1984.

Golant, S.M., "Residential Moves by Elderly Persons to U.S. Central Cities, Suburbs, and Rural Areas," *Journal of Gerontology*, Vol. 42, No. 5, September 1987.

Hanushek, E. and Quigley, J., "Consumption Aspects," in K. Bradbury and A. Downs, eds., *Do Housing Allowances Works?* Brookings Institution, Washington, D.C., 1981.

Institute of Medicine and National Research Council, Committee on an Aging Society, *American's Aging: The Social and Built Environment in an Older Society*, National Academy Press, 1988.

Jacobs, B., "The Elderly—How Do They Fare," in *Measuring Poverty: Scientific Controversy and Political Implications*, D. Besharov, ed., Free Press (forthcoming).

———. "The National Potential of Home Equity Conversion," *The Gerontologist*, Vol. 26, No. 5, October 1986.

———. "Housing Policies for the Elderly," in *Aging: Issues and Policies for the Eighties*, T. Tedrick, ed., Praeger, 1985.

———. "The Potential Antipoverty Impact of RAMs and Property Tax Deferral," *Unlocking Home Equity for the Elderly*, K. Scholen and Y.P. Chen, eds., Ballinger, 1980.

Jacobs, B. and Weissert, W., "Using Home Equity to Pay for Long-Term Care," *Journal of Health Politics, Policy, and Law*, Vol. 12, No. 1, Spring 1987.

Joint Center for Housing Studies, *Homeownership and Housing Affordability in the United States, 1963-85*, Cambridge, MA., 1987.

Lawton, M.P., "Housing Preferences and Choices: Implications" in *Housing an Aging Society*, R.J. Newcomer, et al., eds., Van Nostrant Reinhold, 1986.

Leban, A., "The American Homestead Pogram," *Housing Finance Review*, 3, 1984.

Leutz, W., et al., "Targeting Expanded Care to the Elderly: Early SHMO Experience," *The Gerontologist*, Vol. 28, No. 1, February 1988.

Levy, F., *Dollars and Dreams. The Changing American Income Distribution*, Norton, 1988.

Linneman, P. "The Effect of Rent Control on the Distribution of Income among New York City Renters," *Journal of Urban Economics*, Vol. 22, 1987, pp. 14-34.

Long Term Care Policy Coordinating Council, *Continuing Care Retirement Communities in New York State*, September 1985.

Mills, E.S. and Hamilton, B.W., *Urban Economics*, 3rd Edition, Scott Forseman, 1984.

Mor, V., et. al., "A National Study of Residential Care for the Aged," *The Gerontologist*, Vol. 26, No. 4, August 1986.

National Housing Task Force, "A Decent Place to Live," Washington, D.C., March 1988.

National Association of Realtors, "Home Sales," February 1987.

National Council on Aging, *Aging in the Eighties: America in Transition*, 1981.

Nenno, M., "States Respond to Changing Housing Needs," in "Public Housing: Public Policy in Need of Repair," *The Journal of State Government*, Vol. 60, No. 3, May/June 1987.

New York Economic Development Board, *1978 Official Household Projections for New York State Counties*, March 1978.

New York State Data Center, *Official Population Projections for New York Counties 1980 to 2010*, April 1985.

New York State Department of Housing and Community Renewal, "An Analysis of the Housing Needs for New York State," 1980.

———. Annual Reports, 1982-1988.

New York State Governor's Housing Task Force, *Housing New York, Building for the Future*, December 1988.

New York State Governor's Housing Task Force, *New York State's Housing Programs*, December 1988.

New York State Governor's Office of Management and Productivity, "The Office of Rent Administration: A Management Analysis," November 1987.

New York State Housing Finance Agency, Annual Reports, 1985.

New York State Joint Assembly Committee, "Bleakhouse: DHCR at the Crossroads," June 1987.

New York State Project 2000, "Report on Corrections and Criminal Justice," 1987.

——. "The People of New York: Population Dynamics of a Changing State," 1986.

Newman, S. and Reschovsky, J., "Federal Policy and the Mobility of Older Homeowners," *Journal of Policy Analysis and Management*, Vol. 6, No. 3, 1987.

Oliver, J. and Price, A., "Housing New York's Black Population: Affordability and Adequacy," New York African American Institute, State University of New York, January 1988.

Palmer, J. and Sawhill, I., ed., *The Reagan Experiment*, Urban Institute, Washington, D.C., 1982.

President's National Urban Policy Report, 1984.

Rabushka, A. and Jacobs, B., *Old Folks at Home*, Free Press, 1980.

"Rent Control and New York's Housing Crisis," Manhattan Institute Albany Forum Series, May 6, 1987.

"Report of the Mayor's Blue Ribbon Panel on Building Plan Examination and Review," July 1986.

Reschovsky, J., "Aging in Place: An Investigation into the Housing Consumption and Residential Mobility of the Elderly," working paper, Cornell University.

Rivlin, Alice and Wiener, J., *Reforming Long-Term Care*, The Brookings Institution, 1988.

Roistacher, E. and Tobier E., "Housing Policy," in *Setting Municipal Priorities*, C. Brecher and R. Horton, eds., Allanheld Osman Press, 1984.

——. "Housing Policy," in *Setting Municipal Priorities 1981*, C. Brecher and R. Horton, eds., Allanheld Osman Press, 1980.

Rubinfeld, D. and Wolkoff, M., "The Distributional Impact of Statewide Property Tax Relief: The Michigan Case," *Public Finance Quarterly*, Vol. 11, No. 2, April 1983.

Salins, P.D., "Toward a Permanent Housing Problem," *The Public Interest*, No. 85, Fall 1986, pp. 22-33.

Schnare, A.B., *Externalities, Segregation, and Housing Prices*, Urban Institute, Washington, D.C., 1974.

Scholen, K., et al., *A Financial Guide to the Century Plan*, National Center for Home Equity Conversion, 1984.

Seidel, S., *Housing Costs and Governmental Regulations: Confronting the Regulatory Maze*, Center for Urban Policy Research, 1978.

State of New York Mortgage Agency, Annual Reports, 1981-87.

Statistical Abstract of the United States: 1986, U.S. Governmental Printing Office, 1986.

Stegman, M., *Housing in New York: Study of a City*, 1984.

———. *The Dynamics of Rental Housing in New York City*, Rutger University Press, 1982.

Sternlieb, G. and Hughes, J., "Demographics and Housing in America," *Population Bulletin*, Vol. 41, No. 1, January 1986.

———. *The Future of Rental Housing*, Center for Urban Policy Research, 1981.

Sternlieb, G. and Listokin, D., "Housing," in *Setting Municipal Priorities 1986*, C. Brecher and R. Horton, eds., New York University Press, 1985.

Stone, R., et al., "Caregivers of the Frail Elderly: A National Profile," *The Gerontologist*, Vol. 27, No. 5, October 1987.

Struyk, R., "Home Energy Costs and the Housing of the Poor and the Elderly," in A. Downs, and K. Bradbury, eds., *Energy Costs Urban Development and Housing*, Brookings Institution, Washington, D.C., 1981.

———. "Should Government Encourage Homeownership?" Urban Institute, Washington, D.C., 1977.

Struyk, R.J. and Soldo, B., *Improving the Elderly's Housing*, Ballinger, 1980.

Struyk, R.J. and Turner, M.A., "Changes in the Housing Situation of the Elderly: 1974-79," Urban Institute, 1982.

Talmas, D., "Housing Demand/Needs Analysis of the Impact of the Fort Drum Expansion," Office of Housing and Technical Services, New York State Housing Finance Agency, December 1986.

U.S. Advisory Commission on Intergovernmental Relations, *Significant Features of Fiscal Federalism*.

U.S. Bureau of the Census, *Household Wealth and Asset Ownership: 1984*, Current Population Reports, Series P-70 No. 7, U.S. Government Printing Office, 1986.

———. *Money Income and Poverty Status of Families and Individuals: 1988*,

Current Population Reports, Series P-60 No. 166, October 1989.

U.S. Department of Commerce, Bureau of the Census, *Annual Housing Survey*, New York Standard Metropolitan Statistical Area, 1983.

———. *New York Census of Housing, 1980.*

———. *New York Census of Housing, 1970.*

U.S. Department of Housing and Urban Development, "The Conversion of Rental Housing to Condominiums and Cooperatives," 1980.

Weissert, W., "Estimating the Long-Term Care Population: Prevalence Rates and Selected Characteristics," *Health Care Financing Review*, Vol. 6, Summer 1985.

Weissert, W. and Scanlon, W., "Determinants of Institutionalization of the Aged," Urban Institute Working Paper 1466-20, December 1983.

Wheeler, M., "Resolving Local Regulatory Disputes and Building Consensus for Affordable Housing," MIT Center for Real Estate Development, 1988.

Winklevoss, H. and Powell, A., *Continuing Care Retirement Communities: An Empirical, Financial and Legal Analysis*, Richard D. Irwin, Inc., 1984.

Wiseman, R.E., "Concentration and Migration of Older Americans," *Housing an Aging Society*, R.J. Newcomer et. al., ed., Van Nostrand Reinhold, 1986.

Wolkoff, M.J., "Property Rights to Rent Regulated Apartments: A Path Towards Decontrol," *Journal of Policy Analysis and Management*, Vol. 9, No. 2, Spring 1990.

Name Index

Block, W., 136n.37
Bradbury, K., 138n.56, 139n.70

Clay, P., 143n.145

DiPasquale, D., 134n.15
Downs, A., 133n.9, 138n.56, 139n.70
Durning, D., 139n.72

Felstein, C., 140n.83
Friedman, J., 142n.121

Gantt, D., 139n.79
Garnett, R., 142n.122, 142n.124
Golant, S. M., 143n.138
Guttentag, J., 142n.122, 142n.124

Hanushek, E., 137n.55
Hughes, J., 137n.49

Jacobs, B., 140n.88, 140n.93, 140n.95, 141n.97, 141n.98, 141n.101, 141n.102, 141n.104, 142n.110, 142n.118, 142n.127, 143n.131, 143n.143

Lawton, M., 141n.106
Leutz, W., 143n.137
Levy, F., 133n.2
Linneman, P., 136n.41

Mor, V., 143n.142

Newman, S., 141n.105

Oliver, J., 135n.23
Olsen, E., 136n.37

Palmer, J., 133n.6
Powell, A., 143n.141
Price, A., 135n.23

Quigley, J., 137n.55, 139n.72

Rabushka, A., 141n.97, 141n.98, 141n.101, 141n.104
Reschovsky, J., 141n.105
Rivlin, A., 143n.131
Rubinfeld, D., 139n.69

Salins, P., 134n.17
Sawhill, I., 133n.6
Scanlon, W., 140n.90
Schnare, A. B., 138n.62
Scholen, K., 142n.125
Sjogren, J., 142n.121
Soldo, B., 142n.111
Stegman, M., 136n.38, 136n.39, 140n.83
Sternlieb, G., 137n.49
Stone, R., 140n.91
Struyk, R. J., 138n.62, 139n.67, 142n.111, 142n.115

Talmas, D., 136n.31
Turner, M. A., 142n.115

Subject Index

AARP. *See* American Association of Retired Persons

Abandonment:
effects of maintenance codes on, 83
effects of rent controls on, 48-49
impacts on supply, 83-84
landlord incentives, 83

Accessory Apartments, 124

Activities of Daily Living (ADL), 93-94

Adequacy of Housing (*see also* Housing Quality):
definition of, 16

Affordability (*see also* Cost Gap; Housing Costs):
by income, 35-36, 63-64
by poverty status, 21-23, 35
by region, 36-37
definition of, 34
elderly housing, 103-109
female headed households, 60
HUD guidelines, 33
in New York City, 34
owner cost-to-income ratios, 23, 34
rent-to-income ratios, 27, 51

Affordable Housing (*see also* Cost Gap):
gap, 34-36, 129
shortages, 129
supply by income, 38, 137.45
supply by region, 36-38

Aid to Families with Dependent Children. *See* Federal Housing Policy: and AFDC

Annual Housing Survey of New York City Metropolitan Area, 1983, 34

American Association of Retired Persons, 115

Building Regulations:
code violations, 83
effects on housing costs, 83
effects on housing quality, 83
local building codes, 81-82
maintenance codes, 82-83. *See also* Abandonment
statewide building codes, 9, 148
Uniform Fire Prevention Code, 82

Capital Grants. *See* Housing Subsides

Circuit Breakers. *See* Tax Policy

Cost Gap (*see also* Affordability):
aggregate size, 39, 129
based on median rents, 39-41
based on 25 percentile, 39-41
defined, 38
for owners, 40-43
for renters, 38-40
projections of, 65

Crowding. *See* Housing Quality

Demand Projections (*see also* Supply Projections):
assumptions, 54-55
by region, 56-60
demographic changes, 54-55, 58
explanations for projected increases, 60
for elderly households, 121-122
household composition trends, 60-61
household size, 53, 55
income elasticity of demand, 64
lower household growth assumption, 58
population growth rate, 53
Project 2000 Population Report, 53
relative prices, 58